KAPOHO

Memoir of a Modern Pompeii

KAPOHO

Memoir of a Modern Pompeii

FRANCES H. KAKUGAWA

Most of the names in this book have been changed to protect the privacy of the individuals involved.

ISBN 978-1-9356901-6-0

Library of Congress Control Number: 2011942076

Front cover photo
Shorpy/Vintagraph

Back cover photo
Mary Swisher

Design and production
Gonzalez Design Company

Excerpts from "The Enemy Wore My Face" were previously published in Bamboo Ridge: Journal of Hawai'i Literature and Arts, Issue 9 (1980) and Issue 100 (2011). The author and excerpts also appeared in the film "Black Out Baby."

"Eh, You Tink You Haole?" was first published in Bamboo Ridge Issue 98 (2011) and was the California Writers Club's second-prize winner in 2009.

"You're Going to Hell" was the California Writers Club's first-prize winner in 2009.

"Akira's Flashlight" was the California Writers Club's second-prize winner in 2011.

Watermark Publishing
1088 Bishop Street, Suite 310
Honolulu, Hawai'i 96813
Telephone 1-808-587-7766
Toll-free 1-866-900-BOOK
sales@bookshawaii.net
www.bookshawaii.net

10 9 8 7 6 5 4 3 2 1

Printed in the United States

This book is dedicated to
the memory of my parents
—Sadame and Matsue Kakugawa—
and my grandparents
—Sampachi Kakugawa and Matsuno Ikeda,
Nobuichi and Tsune Takahashi—
and to all my ancestors buried in
Hawaiʻi and in Hiroshima

Also by Frances H. Kakugawa

Sand Grains

White Ginger Blossoms

Golden Spike

The Path of Butterflies

Mosaic Moon: Caregiving through Poetry

Teacher, You Look Like a Horse!

Wordsworth the Poet

Wordsworth Dances the Waltz

Breaking the Silence: A Caregiver's Voice

Contents

Acknowledgments

I am indebted to the many knowledgeable and generous people who have helped bring these stories to you. Each came with so much support and friendship, and I am honored to be in their company.

Red Slider disrupted many a dinner by taking the chopsticks out of my hand and replacing them with a pen, saying, "That makes a good story—write it down now!" Every writer needs an honest and knowledgeable storyteller/collaborator/editor and Red is all of these and more. He knows a good story when he hears one, including those told in Hawai'i pidgin. Thank you for "da kine."

Dr. Charles Pellegrino, author and forensic archaeologist, taught me what excellent writing is through his books and correspondence and inspired me to dig deep under the rocks of Kapoho. Thank you for your support through *omoiyari* and for introducing this book with your Foreword.

J.W. Nicklaus, author and friend, suggested more details to my scenes in his analytical reading of each story. I won't forget that one comparison to Steinbeck! I have not come down yet.

Jennifer Hee, my former third grader, reversed roles and became my mentor. She had the courage to tell me, "You need to work harder to make your stories work" and drove me to rewrite and restructure many of them. I'm still waiting for the day you stop calling me Miss K.

Mary Swisher, professional photographer, author and friend, for her positive reinforcement, editing and for telling me I'd written a good story each time I sent her one. Thank you for the author photo on the back cover, Mary—you have a good camera!

Mark Arax, author and journalist, taught me so much about good writing when he asked me one question: "Do you need that last line?" We do a lot of "Araxing" at my house.

The Sacramento Barnes & Noble writing critique group, led by Norma Jean Thornton, added valuable critique—in addition to tears, laughter and silence—when I shared my rough drafts. Thank you for helping me put commas in all the right places, too. If they're still missing, it's my doing.

The 12th Street Book Club was that rare group of editors who didn't read any of my stories, but whose voices I heard each time I finished a story. "What will they say? Have I over-talked? Do I have a story that will spark a lively discussion of speculation and interest? Or will they show more interest in their dinner?"

Janet Momoe Aoki and Paul Kakugawa received many phone calls when I needed someone to lift the fog from my memories. Janet's story of the Yaito appears in "Mrs. Honda's Beautiful Daughter," while the first permanent she gave me—curling and sizzling my hair around nails heated in a *furo* fire—appears in "The Emperor's Kidnapped Daughter." Paul's story of how he made ashtrays from Pele's lava flows appears in "Once There Was a Kapoho."

Peet's Coffee and Tea on Howe Street in Sacramento was my "writer's cave" where I wrote this book. Anthony Christensen, thank you for the designer cups of decaf latté served in real cups—and saucers, at times.

To my family and the people of Kapoho: My dreams of becoming a writer would not have come to fruition had I lived anywhere else. Thank you for nurturing, supporting and tolerating that "little Kapoho brat" who was so often underfoot.

Thanks also to the Northern California Publishers & Authors, the California Writers Club's Sacramento Branch, the Sacramento Poetry Center and all the readers who continue to ask, "When is your next book coming out?" Thank you for keeping the writer-poet alive in me.

Last but not least, to Watermark Publishing, for presenting my words in a real book in this up-and-coming electronic age—to George Engebretson and Duane Kurisu, for your continued trust in my writing and for preserving the work of writers, and to sales and marketing director Dawn Sakamoto for being totally devoted to working on my behalf. Thank you most sincerely.

Foreword

Decades after the August AD 79 eruption that buried Pompeii and its sister cities, Pliny the Younger chronicled how his beloved neighborhood had disappeared into the earth. Frances Kakugawa is Pliny the Younger to a modern Pompeii called Kapoho.

In the shadow of Vesuvius, Pliny the Younger had come of age after the influx of Buddhist philosophers from the east, and the emergence of new religions that preached similar philosophies—among them, the first Christians. In accordance with a curse that was already ancient in the Far East when Rome was young (a curse cleverly crafted to sound like a blessing at first hearing: *May you live in interesting times*), Pliny was surrounded by nothing except fascinating history.

Frances, too, was surrounded by too much history. Her memories of doomed Kapoho include a birthday party interrupted by a neighbor shouting, "Japan bombed Pearl Harbor!" Her chronicles of Kapoho capture the otherwise forgotten history of growing up as a Japanese American, almost within shouting distance of Pearl Harbor, during the Japanese internment camp period. Frances not only records with sometimes shocking honesty the thoughts of a child coming of age during this period, she captures the color and flavor of lost Kapoho—everything from green beetle hunts and the introduction of Spam to the soldiers who assisted children in Easter egg hunts.

As Frances describes the war years, nothing would ever be the same for the five-year-old with a last name like Kakugawa and a face that, in the eyes of other Americans, "wasn't quite her own." In the backyards of the Kapoho homes, families burned and buried precious heirlooms, porcelain antiques and other mementos from Japan, not wanting to be accused of being disloyal or un-American. Even a small, antique metal horse could arouse suspicion from the Military Police. Years later, believing that the heirlooms had been lost to the ages beneath lava flows, Frances learned from a scientist that the destroyer was also the great preserver: "Kapoho is still there, and always will be there, long after the Sphinx has eroded to dust."

Foreword

From the legends, prayers and ghost stories surrounding the volcano that entombed Frances' town under more than a million tons of lava, to the irony of a family that escaped the war in Japan in general (and Hiroshima in particular) for the illusory peace between Kīlauea and Pearl Harbor, this is a rare, poetic history that will make you smile, think, laugh and cry.

Welcome to the lost world of Kapoho, lovingly unearthed and given new life by Hawaii's Pliny.

Charles Pellegrino
Author, *Ghosts of Vesuvius, The Last Train from Hiroshima*

The Enemy Wore My Face

The Enemy Wore My Face

Under the rising sun,
The enemy came
Wearing my face.

My face changed forever that Sunday afternoon. It seemed a same-same Sunday. My parents were at a neighbor's birthday party, and I was home with my brothers and sister. There were comics on the floor, dishes in the sink and the sense of nothing to do that usually came on the weekends.

Home was Kapoho, a little plantation village near the eastern tip of the Big Island of Hawai'i. Our town was built on the east rift zone of Kilauea, the island's most active volcano. Radios ran on batteries, telephones were almost nonexistent and few of us read the only newspaper on the island, the *Hilo Tribune Herald*. News of the outside world came weeks late through the five-minute newsreels shown before each movie at our generator-run theater. So whatever news caught up with us couldn't be of much consequence. We were always seeing yesterday's news today. When we heard of Joe DiMaggio's 50-game hitting streak, he was already on his 56th. When we heard of Nazi Germany's invasion of Norway and Denmark on April 9, the Germans were already in Belgium and Luxembourg on May 10. That particular Sunday, however, changed everything. Mr. Ito was listening to his radio.

"Japan bombed Pearl Harbor!" he shouted at anyone he saw along the road. "Japan bombed Pearl Harbor!" he shouted at the birthday guests as he rushed on to spread the news. The party immediately broke up, and everyone hurried home.

My father rushed into the house, followed by his neighbors.

"Turn the radio on. Turn the radio on!" Everyone stood in front of the radio, shouting above the crackling voice of the announcer.

"Are you sure he said Japan?"

"Where's Pearl Harbor?"

"This means trouble. This means trouble."

"This means war."

"Are you sure he said Japan?"

I knew something was wrong when no one went into the kitchen to prepare lunch. I was hungry, but no one paid any attention to me. All I heard were arguments and loud voices. That was the day I learned to be afraid. That was the day I learned that there was an enemy, an enemy who would wear my face, an enemy who would not be forgotten or forgiven in the years to come. Shame, humiliation and a host of confused thoughts would now become my shadow. I would hear "Jap" for the first time. We were Americans, I knew that. We were fighting the same enemy, I knew that, too. The face I saw in the mirror looked American to me, and I'd had no reason to believe, up to then, that anyone else saw anything different. The day Mr. Ito went running around the village with the news was the day my face no longer belonged to me.

All of us quickly found out that anything Japanese raised suspicion.

"I'm Japanese?" I asked my mother one day. "I'm not haole?" Such wishful thinking from a five-year-old. The language school was shut down, so I couldn't learn Japanese after school, as my older brother and sister did before the bombing. I attended Kapoho Elementary School, three miles from my house. The army barracks were across from our school. Soldiers, tanks and trucks would come and go, and war seemed always close at hand. The soldiers didn't trouble us, except for the MPs, but neighbors and friends were a problem.

A year after Pearl Harbor, I walked the three miles to school with my head down whenever I passed certain homes. My half-running steps could not escape the "Eh, Jap!" taunts that came from children and adults who wore a different face.

Eh, Jap!

It claws my spine,
Tearing skin.
It enters my body
To devour who I am.

I spit it out! Bull's eye!
So what do you do
With "Eh, Jap!"
On your face?

Mistrust was everywhere in the village air. We, too, harbored our own suspicions. "Be careful of the Filipinos. They carry knives," we were warned by our families. Later I would hear from my Filipino friends. "We were so happy after Pearl Harbor," they confessed. "Until then, the Filipinos were at the bottom of the ladder. Now, the Japanese were at the bottom."

Change came along with blackouts. We spoke in whispers after the sun went down. Our nights were spent huddled around a little wooden box covered with a piece of black-dyed old sheet. Inside the box, a flickering kerosene lamp was the only light in the house. Any glimmer of light outside would give us away. Except for the occasional cry from my baby brother, the house was silent as I sat there in the dark, too scared to say much. The baby, born nine days after December 7, spent most of his time asleep in my mother's arms.

In one corner of the room was a paper carton of clothes and evacuation necessities, a daily reminder of the war. The battery-run radio was turned on only for news. I fidgeted with nervousness whenever I heard the announcer's voice relaying war news with a reminder to stay tuned for emergency bulletins. I didn't quite understand what he was saying, but I knew from the tone of his voice that it was something to be afraid of. My reaction to male radio newscasters, who spoke in robotic voices without much inflection, would follow me long into my adult life, as a forecast impending disaster.

Villagers began to build their own air-raid shelters after December 7. One of our neighbors had a shelter dug and cemented with railroad ties at the entrance, which was camouflaged with bushes. Some neighbors spoke of sharing their shelters with other neighbors.

We played in those shelters feeling the cold dampness of the dirt floors and smelling the mildew growing on the walls. In a corner, boxes of canned goods would be piled: Spam, sardines, pork and beans, Saloon Pilot crackers and Libby's corned beef. I hated to go into those shelters, yet I couldn't refuse to follow my friends. I felt the fear of war when we played in them. We didn't have a shelter of our own. I never questioned my parents when they spoke of the cave in my grandmother's backyard. She lived about six miles away. "We will use that," they said, "in case of an attack." But I wanted a shelter of my own. I felt unprotected and scared. I feared I was going to be the first to die when the bombs fell. I wanted to be safe like the other children with their own shelters. I didn't want to die.

After the day the world changed, Sundays held a special apprehension. On one of those Sundays, an uncle drove up in his old clunky Ford, shouting, "Turn the radio on! Turn the radio on. Air attack! We might have air attack!"

The five children were hastily stuffed in the back seat of his car. Futon after futon was piled on top of us. I couldn't see a thing as the car sped down the bumpy road to our grandmother's. The ride was long and silent. I was too scared to cry. I wanted a shelter like my friends, but I was taught not to complain. Later, we sat in the living room, huddled around the radio. To reassure themselves, the adults kept murmuring over and over, "It will clear, it will clear." The children sat in silence waiting for the attack to come. After what seemed hours, the All Clear finally came over the radio.

War followed us into our classroom. Each day our lessons began with the Pledge of Allegiance and the Pearl Harbor Song. I learned this song during my first week of school. It was mandatory.

The Pearl Harbor Song

History in every century
Records an act that lives forevermore.
We'll recall, as into line we fall,
The thing that happened on Hawaii's shore.

Chorus:
Let's remember Pearl Harbor
As we go to meet the foe.
Let's remember Pearl Harbor
As we did the Alamo.

We will always remember
How they died for liberty.
Let's remember Pearl Harbor
And go on to victory.

War changes everything. Even the most innocent childhood games are redirected to that dark effort. We dyed eggs the night before the first Easter after Pearl Harbor. We drew pictures on eggs with crayons and dipped them in a dye made by boiling skins of yellow onions. The next day, the teachers would hide the eggs in the schoolyard for the great Easter egg hunt. A stone wall bordered the front of the school. Soldiers sat on it, watching us, pointing and telling us where to look for the eggs. The young women teachers appeared to be irritated. During the egg hunt, I forgot about war, but only for an hour. The sight of the soldiers left fear inside of me, the fear of war.

At the end of the day, we exchanged our eggs for oranges and apples, which the soldiers always seemed to have in abundance. Often, they tossed fruit to us from the back of their moving trucks. I must have looked like those pictures of children from war-torn countries of today, barefooted in a home-sewn dress that hung loosely below my knees, staring at them, a bit bewildered. Soldiers meant guns, enemies and death. Yet the soldiers we met brought with them their own brand of kindness and friendliness by helping us find our Easter eggs and tossing us fruit.

Our curriculum also changed. We spent a few hours each day doing work for the American Red Cross. We sat on the classroom floor cutting fabric into little pieces. My mother was a seamstress, so she gave me scraps of leftover material, which I proudly took to school. Our cuttings were sent to the army hospitals as filler for pillows for wounded soldiers. The work gave me a feeling that I was doing something for my country. My fingers were covered with blisters, but patriotism was a strong, almost romantic impulse, and blisters were a small sacrifice.

"I'm cutting this for a handsome, blue-eyed solder in a hospital," I told a classmate sitting next to me.

She giggled and said, "Me, too. Mine has red hair."

"Let's write our name on a piece of paper and put it in the pile. Maybe they will write to us."

We hastily wrote our names on scraps of paper and hid them in the piles of cut fabric. If we had had telephones, I probably would have included my phone number. One day my sense of patriotism was so intense that I snipped pieces off the hem of my cotton dress, thinking it would be my ultimate sacrifice to that wounded soldier somewhere.

"What have you done?" The teacher's angry voice interrupted my reverie. I got a good rap on the knuckles that day for being a patriot. I was in the second grade.

The war went on and so did the romance. The Japanese Language School was converted into a USO hall. We knew exactly when to be there to watch the USO girls entertaining the soldiers. We stared through the windows or sat in the doorway. Sometimes the USO girls would motion the soldiers to bring us cookies and juice.

I doubted the conversations I overheard among the ladies in the village. "The USO girls are a bad influence on our young girls. Look at them, so wild and wicked with red-painted nails and high heels."

"What do they know," I'd say, as I sneaked off to the USO hall.

Too young to entertain soldiers, I discovered a secret way to help them. My sister pointed it out to me one day. "When you see these green bugs that look like a fan, kill them. These are Japanese bugs. We can win the war if we kill them. Each time you kill one, the Japanese army gets weaker."

I searched for those bugs and crushed them under my bare feet.

"There," I'd say. "Die so we can win the war." This was exhilarating and easier than entertaining soldiers, though painted red nails would always be kept on my wish list. I was too young to wonder what my grandmothers were thinking when they saw us killing insects to help defeat the army of Emperor Hirohito. They still loved and honored the emperor whom they had left behind when they had migrated to Hawai'i.

Killing of the Bugs

Hirohito weakens
In the crush of green bugs
Under my bare feet.
The Rising Sun is setting.

Later, I would learn that while I was slaughtering bugs, a future sister-in-law and her friends in Japan were throwing rocks at an American soldier's uniform filled with straw and hung from a tree. It was their daily ritual as they walked to and from school.

I went to bed every night during the war years with a special prayer on my lips. One might have expected that I prayed for our soldiers. But it wasn't for the soldiers. "Please, God," I prayed, "Keep me alive, don't make me die. Let me live until the seventh grade."

When I pulled weeds in our vegetable garden, I would pray the same prayer. Why seventh grade? Because that was the year I would attend Pāhoa High and Intermediate School on a bus. I could wear shoes to school for the first time. I was promised my first hair permanent, not a homemade job like the ones I secretly did by curling strands around a hot nail with its sizzle of burnt hair. It would be a real permanent, and maybe I would get some red nail polish, too. No war was going to deprive me of these spoils of growing up. So I prayed every day to be alive for a few more years. I promised God I would be good. That, and I continued to kill those green bugs.

The local men were trained to guard and patrol the village. They marched in the ballpark, keeping time as soldiers do, following their leader with shortened broomsticks slung over one shoulder. They were so disciplined and earnest that one day I watched them march right up to the top of a high woodpile that stood in the middle of the park. There was no way down the other side, so they simply continued to march in place. The leader had failed to give them instructions to turn right or left. After that, we played "soldiers" too, marching in straight lines, purposely instructing ourselves not to turn right or left until we faced the wall of a house and stood there marching in place.

Mr. Naka, an elderly Japanese neighbor who spoke no English, would stop and salute every soldier he met in the village. One day I saw him by his gate in his white boxer shorts, saluting soldiers. My friends and I followed him around, making fake salutes and laughing behind his back. Mr. Naka would be the first villager to lose a son in the war.

One night the silence of our house was shattered by a gunshot. "What's that? We're being attacked!" It was only the sound of a rock thrown on our corrugated roof. We shook with fright. It was the blackout watchman warning us—we had to be careful of lights that glowed from our kerosene lamps. Soldiers and village men patrolled the roads. Each night my father took a walk around the outside of our house to check to see if any rays of light were coming through the cracks. We filled the cavities from the inside with putty.

Any light seen at night would draw enemy planes to bomb the village. We were a prime target because of our light—the Kapoho lighthouse—a beacon for ships passing Kapoho Lookout Point. We had to protect this light by living in the darkness. But how could darkness mean safety? I didn't feel safe in the dark. Just more exposed, more vulnerable.

Making matters worse were the gas masks. They were ugly, heavy masks with a strong rubbery and medicinal odor. They came in green canvas bags that we were forced to sling over our shoulders each time we left the house. Infants, like my baby brother, could not use them. It would be a while before they found a way of protecting babies. My mother never took her gas mask with her. She said she would not carry a gas mask until my brother was protected, too. He soon received one in the form of a sleeping bag.

"Gas mask drill! Gas mask drill!" It was time for another war-related exercise in school. The masks were periodically checked for leaks. A classroom was filled with tear gas.

"All right, children. On the count of three, put your masks on. You must do this in less than five seconds. One! Two! Three!" I opened the snap on my canvas bag, took out my mask and pulled it over my face, starting with the chin. I found problems breathing in the rubbery smell of the mask. My heart beat like bumblebee wings.

Then, like cattle to a slaughterhouse, we tiny little aliens entered the tear-gassed room. I felt less frightened on days when my older brother was a monitor. He walked over to each of us, checking our faces.

"No tears, no tears," he announced.

If a mask leaked, it was quickly replaced.

There were evacuation practices as well. We were timed walking from school to home with soldiers following us in their army trucks. I hated these sessions. It made the war seem so close. I felt safer in school with all the children and teachers and distractions. Teachers seemed indestructible.

One thing the army didn't supply. We all carried it in little home-sewn bags around our necks. It was a piece of camphor-like asafetida for protecting us against germs. Word was that the soldiers carried germs. It was a bit of homegrown magic added to my daily prayers. Maybe I would live to attend the seventh grade after all.

My father befriended four soldiers who often visited during their off-duty hours. One soldier, an Italian, craved spaghetti. He and my mother worked in the kitchen, and he showed her how to cook real pasta. It was a common sight to come home and see the soldiers playing cards in our living room. My father's younger sister, Ma-chan, lived with us then. She was regarded as a great beauty in the village. Perhaps that was why the soldiers came to visit. The night before the soldiers shipped out, they had her stand in front of them to be admired. I looked on with envy, wondering when it would be my turn. For three of the soldiers, it would be their last look at a beautiful woman.

Often we saw truckloads of soldiers being transferred to the war front. One day, an army truck stopped briefly by our yard, long enough to roll a large wooden barrel from the back. Without a word, they waved goodbye and drove off. We were scared, and my mother warned us to stay away from the barrel until my father returned. "It might be explosives," someone said. When my father came home, he opened it carefully. It was filled with white flour, a luxury.

"This must be from the four soldiers," my father explained, "to thank us for the spaghetti."

"Hubba hubba," "soldier bait" and "soldier babies" became part of my childhood vocabulary. Hapa-haole babies born in Kapoho during the war were accepted with the same affection that would be given to any child. That is, except for the silence surrounding their origin. My father would recall the story of a young husband greeting his new hapa-haole son:

"He walked around his newborn son saying, 'Huh? You got blue eyes? Huh? You soldier baby, huh?' as he lifted him into his arms."

My father often told stories of these "soldier babies" concluding with, "It was a good thing my daughters were all too young for soldiers." He'd laugh when I'd respond, "What a shame. I would be a captain's or general's wife today!"

Soldiers were one thing. The MPs were quite another. Searches for disloyalty were synonymous with "Military Police" and their red and white armbands. They entered our houses unannounced, searching for any sign of loyalty to Japan. Our loyalty to America didn't seem to matter. Homes with issei residents were searched for books, herbs, personal documents, anything that might connect them to the emperor. Such items were confiscated. Men were taken away to internment camps. Families were broken.

"Did you hear that Mr. Miura was taken away during the night?" villagers whispered among themselves. "Not good to be a Japanese-language teacher right now," they added.

Conversations were held in whispers. Silence ruled the Japanese households of Kapoho. We were the enemy now.

Though my parents were nisei, born in Hawai'i, they took no chances and destroyed all our Japanese records, books, toys and anything else that might "smell Jap." We spent hours tearing the red dots off our Japanese medicine packages. My parents were afraid that these dots might be mistaken for symbols of the rising sun.

One family changed their diet from rice to spaghetti to become more American. For them, even rice had turned into red dots.

There were many bonfires in the backyards of Kapoho. Ours as well. People burned family heirlooms, antiques and irreplaceable treasures they had brought from Japan. Day and night, the burning went on to hide our ancestry.

One item that probably should have gone to the bonfire somehow escaped. It was a small horse sculpted in metal. It was treasured by my parents for its resemblance to Emperor Hirohito's horse. He was often photographed on his horse during the war. The connection was remote; who would associate a metal horse with some threat to our country?

What backyard bonfires couldn't erase, Pele, the goddess of fire, would come to claim 14 years later. She put to rest all our burnt artifacts and memories under a blanket of lava. During the relocation of the remaining village to a new site several miles away, somehow the horse was saved and returned to its place of prominence on the shelf in our house.

Fire

During the fires of Pele,
Kapoho evacuated.
In the bonfires of things Japanese,
My ancestors struggled to remain.

In one respect, we were better off than most. We were poor to begin with, so restrictions and rations were taken for granted. We still had our Spam, Vienna sausage and rice.

My father planted a garden as a defense against days when food was scarce. We had abundant peanuts and sweet potatoes in our garden. He continued to fish, but the war brought a few new demands. My mother stood in line for liquor and cigarette permits. I would watch our teenage neighbor climb into the back of a truck every morning with her hoe and gloves. She belonged to the Victory Corps and grew extra produce for the war effort. After awhile, life became routine under the threat of air raids and bombs. We were still treated like the enemy at times, but we felt American.

Our 18-year-old neighbor Taro Naka came to say goodbye after being drafted. "I'll return a lieutenant," he proudly told my mother. His issei parents proudly displayed a photo of Taro in his private-first-class uniform. An American flag was next to it.

A few months later, Taro did come back. He was still a private.

"How can I be sure it's my son in the coffin when it's closed?" Mrs. Naka asked, looking at the flag-draped casket. Mrs. Naka was a Buddhist. She wanted to hold a wake with an open casket to be sure that her son was truly dead before the burial. Rumors were that many of these caskets were being returned empty. The two soldiers who had accompanied the casket remained silent.

The neighborhood women had gathered at the home to prepare food for the funeral. Rice balls sprinkled with black sesame seeds were round instead of the usual triangular shape. There would be no meat. Women kept counting the ingredients in each dish and the number of dishes on the table.

All even numbers were considered symbols of death.

"Should we feed the soldiers?"

"Yes, see if they eat Japanese food."

My mother, the only English-speaking woman in the kitchen, took two platefuls of food to the soldiers while the other women peeked through the half-closed door. Giggles followed as they observed the soldiers finishing their food.

"Not bad for haole soldiers. They're eating our food."

"They must be hungry."

More giggles filled the kitchen when one of the soldiers gave his empty plate to my mother and asked, "How did you stick the seeds on the rice?"

She later told the ladies in Japanese, "I should have said we use spit."

This conversation was repeated throughout the years to come, as people looked back with humor on a day filled with grief.

My Uncle Shun was also drafted. For years, I'd heard the village argument that Roosevelt took us into war. By the time Uncle Shun was drafted, I had figured it out. Without a president of the United States, there would be no war. Uncle Shun was a soldier now. I also knew that the first thing a soldier did was to go visit the president in the White House. It would be simple, I thought, for Uncle Shun to end this war. All he needed to do was to kill the president. Throughout Uncle Shun's years in the army, I kept hoping for such an end.

The Day Uncle Shun Ended the War

The soldiers are standing.
In walks the president.
"Hello, soldiers," he says.

Uncle Shun, in the third row,
Takes aim and shoots.
The war is over.

The war did not end. Roosevelt was still president. Uncle Shun was still a soldier, and I continued to kill the green bugs.

Then one day, an issei neighbor appeared at our door. "*Zuluzulubelu ga shinda,*" she called. "*Zuluzulubelu ga shinda,*" Roosevelt has died. With a sigh of relief, she added, "Maybe the war will now end." All day, there were happy and hopeful sounds in the village. "*Zuluzulubelu ga shinda*. Maybe the war will end."

The war didn't end. Soldiers died. Internment camps filled. Uncle Shun was still in the army. And we were still "Japs."

I remember little about the end of the war. My illusion of ending the war with Uncle Shun's deed must have been shattered. Whatever other thoughts I may have had about ending the war were consumed in a flash so bright that I would forget everything else. My history was erased on both sides of the Pacific. Both of my faces had been vaporized.

Hiroshima

We sliced the chrysanthemum
Off its stalk
And left it naked in the sun.

The bombing of Hiroshima was the cause of many loud discussions in our house. My father never heard from any of his relatives again. Some of my mother's relatives survived, but it would be some time before she knew what had happened to them. Years later, my father would question my mother about sending money or clothing to her family in Hiroshima. It was painful that he could not do the same for his own family. My mother had spent part of her early childhood in Hiroshima because her family had needed to take her ailing father back to Japan. He had died when she was three, and she had returned to Hawai'i a few years later with her remaining family. My father had visited Hiroshima as a young man. My grandparents on both sides of my family had been born in Hiroshima. Their history was gone for good.

In 1989, I taught a third-grade student from Hiroshima. Noriyo and her family had just moved to Hawai'i with her grandmother. Her grandmother had been exposed to radiation during the bombing. Now, some 44 years later, her physician had recommended that she move to Hawai'i for its gentler climate to help ease the pain of her cancer-ridden body.

44 Years Later

A dark mushroom cloud
Follows me across the Pacific
Into my classroom.

Forgive us, Noriyo,
For Hiroshima
And Nagasaki.

The end of the war filled our kitchen with noisy arguments for quite some time. My father's nisei voice rose above those of his friends over the question of who had won the war. It was the same old argument. The first-generation men insisted that Japan had won the war. The second-generation men maintained otherwise. The Japanese-American soldiers who had fought in the famed 442nd Regimental Combat Team and 100th Infantry Battalion of the army were all nisei. I am certain none of the old issei of Kapoho ever told them that Japan had won the war!

I thought these were the passing arguments of old men who drank too much beer or saké late into the night. One day, however, my 88-year-old grandmother came running up the gravel road to our house, panting with excitement. She kept calling for my mother. I rushed out to greet her. "Hi, Oba-ban."

"I heard from the emperor!
I heard from the emperor!"
The Japanese words tumbled out of her mouth.
"He called and said
Japan won the war!
Isn't that wonderful?"
Her eyes, her smile,
Ecstatic with joy.

"Oba-ban, Oba-ban,"
I said in English,
"Japan surrendered
Thirty-five years ago."

My grandmother's delusions startled me. Did this mean that for the past 35 years, my grandmother had lived in an unresolved war? Had she finally reconciled this only through some magical communication? I looked at her and wondered, "What do I know about losing the pride of one's homeland and one's emperor?"

Along with my parents, Oba-ban always referred to Emperor Hirohito by his title. "*Tennou-heika sama,*" "The Honorable Emperor."

"Hey, Hirohito, nice horse," I would say, just to get a rise out of my mother. "*Bachi ga ataru,*" she'd snap back. "You'll get punished."

Decades after the end of the war, Emperor Hirohito did pay a visit to Hawai'i. News of this came by way of a close friend:

> "My 90-year-old grandmother," she said, "who is fragile and weak in her legs, insisted on seeing the emperor. I argued with her,

'Grandma, you'll have to stand in the hot sun for hours to wait for the motorcade. We can watch it on TV.' She wouldn't hear of that and insisted on seeing the emperor for herself.

"It took me over two hours to prepare her for the visit. She wanted to take a bath, wash her hair and have it blow-dried. She refused to wear a mu'umu'u. It would have been so easy to throw a mu'umu'u over her head, but no, she insisted on stockings and a dress. I ran two pairs of stockings, just trying to put them on her arthritic legs. Luckily, one of her dresses reserved for funerals still fitted her. I made a few quick purchases, a pair of black shoes and a small clutch bag for her handkerchief and wallet.

"We stood in the hot sun on the sidewalk for nearly an hour, waiting for the emperor's motorcade. Grandma refused to sit on a chair that I had brought with us.

"'No one sits in the presence of the Emperor,' she said, in a tone that suggested her daughter had failed to raise me properly. As the motorcade slowly approached, I said, 'Look, Grandma, the emperor is coming.'

"I climbed on the chair to take a good look for myself. Goodness, he was just a shadow of a little man with a tiny moustache, dressed in a black suit on a hot summer's day. The red carnation lei was bigger than his shoulders. All this fuss over that? I looked at my grandmother as he passed. She was standing there with her head bowed low and her hands pressed together. I heard her whispering, '*Tennou-heika sama. Tennou-heika sama.*'"

Emperor Hirohito's Visit to Hawai'i

A sansei, in denim jeans and zoris,
Meets the eyes of the emperor;
An issei bows, seeing only her own feet
As the emperor passes by.

My dreams during and after those years were huge. I wanted to become a writer, a war correspondent like Margaret Higgins or Ernie Pyle. It was a favorite pastime of mine to sign my name alongside that of Higgins or Pyle. I, too, would become a writer, I thought. Books would be the only survivors of civilization, and I wanted to survive at least with my name on a book cover, if nothing else. I wanted to believe that I would live happily ever after. I read a lot. It was a good escape from a world that made no sense. Sometimes that is all there is for a child thrown into a world of constant change—a world of fear and destruction interlaced with her own ignorance.

Pearl Harbor was bombed on December 7. The copy of my first published book of poems arrived on December 7. Today, I sometimes see myself in the photos of children in the news media. The enemy continues to wear the face of children who will kill their own green bugs and end wars. We live our double-faced lives. My face is their face.

My name is either Hideko Frances Kakugawa or Frances Hideko Kakugawa, depending on what document I am holding. My birth certificate carries the name my parents gave me and tells one story. My Social Security card bears the American name first and tells another. Either way, the history of the young girl I would have become is gone. The only face that was left for me to wear was my own.

Portrait

A crayoned flag
Of red, white and blue
Waves from a chopstick
Clutched in my hand.

In the other,
The emperor's chrysanthemum
On a rice-paper fan
Covering half my face. ▣

Eh! You Tink You Haole?

"Eh! You tink you haole?" This was the ultimate put-down. "You think you're white?" Whites were the plantation managers in our village, movie stars, mainlanders and fancy-dressed city slickers. They spoke proper English, were well mannered, sat at tables covered with white linen tablecloths, used napkins instead of sleeves, and ate with forks, spoons and knives, and by candlelight. We were locals.

Pidgin has limitless ways to say exactly what we want to:

"What? You tink you fut perfume? You think you shit ice cream?" Haoles did both, of course. By candlelight, they were an evolutionary step beyond us.

We have a saying in Hawai'i: "Put a bunch of crabs in a bucket, and when one tries to climb out, the others will pull it down."

I planned to get out of Kapoho to reach that star I'd hung my dream on since first grade. It was a very deep bucket, but I was going to get out. But how was I going to become a great writer with a mouthful of pidgin? I had to start speaking "like a haole." That would mean being different. That would mean, "Eh, you tink you haole?"

My earliest recollection of the printed word was when I was five years old. I watched my oldest brother go through the *Hilo Tribune Herald*, turning the pages without reading each article.

"How come he not reading every word? If I know how to read, I goin' read every word." I later took the newspaper and read all the "the" words. "The" was the only printed word I knew.

I learned to read in first grade—that is, more than "the." I was delighted. It was pure magic to read about Dick, Jane and Sally with Spot and Sally's teddy bear Tim. I could read! I ached for their little red wagon, a wish I held throughout my childhood years. In the end, I had to settle for red Saturns and Hondas. Life-changing magic happened one day in first grade. I heard my first poem. The teacher read a poem about flowers speaking to each other. I saw visions of flowers with faces painted with long black eyelashes and red smiling lips. I was totally captivated. I fell in love with words and their magic and vowed that I would someday become a writer.

I read a lot. I immersed myself in the world of language. I wanted something more than Kapoho, and language was my ticket. I had to learn to speak correctly if I were to follow my dream. I would be different. It was my secret, and I never explained it to anyone.

The boys in my classroom read my silence and understood my dream. Instead of putting me down for "talking like a haole," they surprised me. Each time I spoke in Standard English, they told me, "Yeah, you goin' college."

My face was often in a book, and I seldom joined my classmates in games. The boys said, "She goin' college." The girls shook their heads and left me alone.

On the last day of sixth grade, a group of boys watched me walk out of the school grounds, and I heard one voice yell, "Hey, college girl, you goin' college, man." My heart inflated like a balloon that never popped until I took Speech 101 in college. One of the boys was 16 years old. He wasn't going to college; he wasn't even going to junior high. He had waited to be 16 so that by law, he could drop out of school.

Talking haole is easier said than done. My three teachers from the first through sixth grades were high school graduates from the village, without college degrees. They read to us daily and tried anything and everything to help us grow beyond the limited world of Kapoho.

Our homes had no telephones, so in school, the teachers used role-playing to teach us telephone etiquette.

"Hello."

"Hello. May I speak to John, please?"

"One moment, please."

Instead of:

"Eh, I like talk to John."

"Wait, eh, I go call 'em."

Teachers brought in olives and cheese to give us a taste for haole cuisine. I met a teacher 40 years later, and she told her own story of being shocked that many of her students had never tasted olives. Olives would later become "holiday food" on Christmas and New Year's Day.

Two words tripped me up constantly and became my nemesis: "hospital" and "volcano." I added extra syllables to them. "Her father was ill so he went to the 'ha-see-pee-tall'" and "The 'vo-lo-cay-no' is erupting." Each time I mispronounced these words, my name went up in lights on the blackboard. At the end of the day, there was a tally after my name for all mispronounced words.

I stayed after school and pronounced each word 20 times for each tally. "Volcano, volcano, volcano, hospital, hospital, hospital..." The following day, "ha-see-pee-tall" and "vo-lo-cay-no" came rolling off my tongue, uncontrollable lava, heated with frustration.

I spent many afternoons repeating these words over and over again, but the "th" sound was my Everest.

"Stick your tongue out between your teeth when you say the 'th' sound in 'the, there, this, father, mother,'" the teacher instructed. I placed my tongue between my teeth, pulled it back in and said, "Da, dere, dis, fadda, madda." I stuck my tongue out a lot learning to speak right. I didn't mind. I was learning to speak haole, where my dreams lived.

I began my freshman year at the two-year University of Hawai'i campus in Hilo. Making a living now had to be part of the mix of becoming a writer. A detour through the College of Education seemed the best way to do both.

But my Standard English interlaced with pidgin created an insurmountable barrier to my career plans. The University of Hawai'i required that we pass the Speech Board to qualify for other speech courses as a prerequisite to enrolling in the College of Education. Bonehead Speech 100 was my first stop.

After Speech 100, I faced the Speech Board at the end of the semester and failed. My pidgin dialect gave me away. I stood there dumbfounded. After all my years of practice, I still couldn't speak like a haole. I should have taken up accounting.

A board member from the Mānoa campus on O'ahu suggested that I attend a speech clinic for a semester and try again. He gave me his home telephone number and said, "Call me when you transfer to the main campus."

I transferred to the main campus, attended the speech clinic and once again stood before the Speech Board. One of the board members (not my friend, of course) burst into laughter after my short speech. "My God," he said, "How did she end up with a Southern accent?"

"Oh, shit," I thought frantically. "Now I have two dialects!"

The tutor at the speech clinic was from the South. The board members conferred and let it go; I was headed for Speech 105. Whew! I left before they could change their minds. I walked toward the door, turned around and said, "Bye, y'all," and smiled back at them. Some students weren't as fortunate and were forced to switch career plans.

Three and a half years after receiving my teaching degree, I taught for a year at a Michigan elementary school. Faculty members were intrigued by my New England dialect. I was a carrier of Hawai'i's history of missionaries who had arrived from New England after Captain Cook. At the end of the school year, the principal confessed that a teacher had been assigned to observe me because my first graders were the best behaved, and the other faculty members were interested in my technique. "It was your use of language," the principal said.

"Our kids are always rowdy after recess. We watched you stand at the door after recess. You just point your thumb toward your door and quietly say, 'In' or 'Recess is over.' Your kids all settle down and walk in quietly. It was the same at assemblies and on field trips. Your students are the best behaved."

The entire faculty, I learned, began to speak in shorter sentences instead of rambling on and on about how recess was over and the children needed to get into the classroom. She chuckled, "We learned not to over-talk because kids stopped listening to us, but we noticed, as the year went along, that your sentences were getting longer as ours got shorter." Was I finally speaking like a haole?

After I returned to Hawai'i, a debate on pidgin versus Standard English plagued me during my years of teaching.

"No! No! No!" argued the linguists. "A dialect ought not to be tampered with and should be part of our language in and out of school."

"It might save the culture," I replied, "but it didn't save me." I wouldn't allow pidgin in my classroom. My students were free to speak any language or dialect outside of the classroom. But I was determined not to have any Speech Board crush the aspirations of my students. Not on my watch. The linguists need not have worried. My native use of pidgin still screws me up. And my sentences are as short as ever.

Five years ago, I returned to the Islands for a funeral. Three old Kapoho friends came up to me after the service.

"Eh, you da Kakugawa girl, eh?"

"Eh, we read about you all da time. We have all your books, you know."

"We so proud of you. Man, you some famous. We see you on TV all da time."

"No, not famous," I said. "And hey, we all came from the same outhouse." We laughed and talked story about Kapoho and the good old days before it was destroyed by lava.

One of these old friends had a special place in my heart. He had lifted me up to the rim of the bucket. "Go speak like one haole," he had said, "because you goin' college."

The Kindergarten Dropout of Kapoho

I was a kindergarten dropout. There was no other choice—it was either drop out of kindergarten or go to jail for the rest of my life.

On the first day of school, students were running around the classroom. My neighbor Sammy was on top of a table trying to escape the teacher. I was envious as he leaped from table to table, Gene Kelly fashion, laughing and having the time of his life. Other kids were running around the lower decks, knocking down chairs and playing tag. In the free-for-all room, I stood like a statue, wishing I could be running around. This would not be the first time I would feel inadequate, that I was not being raised right by my parents.

"How come I don't know how to run around like Sammy?" But before I could find an answer, fear overtook me and froze me in my chair. The person I had learned to fear most stood in the doorway.

I watched the teacher approach the silhouette in the doorway. They spoke in muted tones to each other. They turned back toward the class, and I felt their eyes on me. He had come for me.

"Why dey lookin' at me? He goin' take me to jail." The fear of the policeman accompanied me for the rest of the day. I needed to get out of there. I wanted to go home. He was taking me to jail. That was what policemen did. I wanted my mother.

Kindergarten was not compulsory in the 1940s. Pāhoa School was seven miles from where we lived. They added kindergarten classes for the first time that year, and I became the first victim. My mother offered me a bribe I couldn't refuse.

"Oh, you're so lucky," my mother said. "You and Sammy will be the first two from Kapoho to go to kindergarten. How lucky. You'll get to ride the bus with all the big people."

"No, I not going. I staying home with you."

"You can wear a new dress every day,"

It would mean riding the Higashi bus, which made one daily round trip from Kapoho to Hilo. We would be dropped off at Pāhoa School and picked up in the afternoon, which meant that I would be stuck in school for the whole day with no way to escape. It also meant that I would be riding with adults and older students whom I didn't know and didn't want to know.

"No, I staying home."

"You're a big girl. You can play with other children in school."

"I no like be big," I flatly stated.

She took out the Sears catalog and showed me dresses from the children's section.

"Here, I will sew you all these dresses. Look how pretty. You can wear a new dress every day."

Like mother, like daughter; female vanity kicked in. I was a goner and succumbed to the bribe. I realized my big mistake only after I got on the bus. I felt like a little weed in a field of wildflowers. People were talking and laughing, visiting with each other. No one spoke to me. I couldn't see Sammy. I sat there scared that the bus would take me to Hilo and I would be lost forever. I should have stayed home.

When the bus dropped us off, an older student accompanied Sammy and me to class. I was too scared to admire my new dress and tagged along after Sammy like Mary's little lamb.

That first day of kindergarten came and went. I knew I would not return, and no Sears catalog could make me change my mind. My mother tried everything but failed to get me back on that bus.

After a few weeks, the Sears catalog came out again, and the bribe was larger this time.

"I'll sew you matching schoolbags for each of your dresses. I'll sew you many many new dresses." This time her bribe didn't work; I was, by now, a more experienced five-year-old. I shook my head. All the dresses in the world would not stop policemen from dragging me to jail. I wasn't going, and that was final.

This wasn't the first time I had learned about fear. It had happened with Sammy's father when I was three. I was standing on our front porch when Sammy's father walked past with a burlap bag slung over his shoulder. He was on his way to the beach.

"I'm going to catch you and put you in my bag," he teased, but I took him seriously and ran into the house.

"I made a big mistake," I heard him tell my parents. "She always runs when she sees me now. We really need to be careful what we say to the children. She's still afraid of me."

Burlap bags and policemen were scary things, always tempting me to hide in the attic for good—that is, if we had had one.

The lures and the bribes continued, but I knew better. The kindergarten teacher sent a note through Sammy: "Please return to school. We miss you."

Sammy dropped by to show me his artwork. "If you come back, you can make dis, too."

"No," I said, sitting on the porch, "I have to stay home. My father miss me." My father cut cane all day long. His five-year-old daughter's absence was of no importance. But that was my answer, and I wouldn't budge.

That Easter, Sammy showed me his Easter basket. It was made out of colored construction paper, filled with artificial grass and multicolored candy eggs. I was filled with envy, but I refused to return to a place where policemen were waiting for me with handcuffs. I didn't need to attend school to learn what they did to children.

"If you not good, I calling the policeman to take you away to jail." It was a standard threat in Sammy's family. His mother used it whenever she needed to discipline him. Not that it did any good in Sammy's case. Sammy never bought into the threat. He continued to get into trouble. Once we played cops and robbers, and Sammy said, "You're the bad guy," and stabbed my sister in her hand with his pocketknife.

Sammy's mother cleaned and bandaged my sister's wound with alcohol, threatening Sammy, "I callin' the police. You goin' jail for this."

It was an idle threat. Never happened, not once. But it took residence in my head. Schoolrooms with policemen in the doorway were no place for five-year-olds with a passionate desire to stay out of jail. I dropped out of kindergarten; the risk wasn't worth a busload of new dresses with matching schoolbags. Not to this Kapoho girl. ▣

Speaker of the House

My first day of school was less threatening this time. My sister Momoe and brother Sada were accompanying me on the three-mile walk to Kapoho School. I felt protected and safe. They wouldn't let anything bad happen to me.

I was dressed in a new red and white checkered dress, a style I had selected from the Sears catalog. It was a dress a notch above the Sears dress because my mother had added red rickrack around the edges of the white Peter Pan collar and the puffed sleeves. The slightly flared skirt made it easy to whirl like a dancer. A sash attached at the side of my waist was neatly tied in the back with a tight bow. I had a matching bag with the same red rickrack stitched on the strap.

"Momoe has the same dress as you, so if you want to find her at recess, look for a girl who has the same dress as you." I felt reassured by my mother's words after becoming a kindergarten dropout the previous year. I was ready for first grade.

"No policeman," I thought, after casing the joint as we walked through the school entrance between two concrete walls. Four brown buildings greeted us.

"That's your room," Momoe said, pointing to the building on the left. A staircase led to the one-room classroom that housed the first and second graders.

"I'm next to you in that low building, and Sada's is next to mine." The staircase to his room was higher than the first building.

"See that cottage? That's the cafeteria, where we go to pick up our lunch." The tour was over, and we went our separate ways to our classrooms.

I felt a sense of relief when the teacher assigned me a seat next to Sammy Kahele and Kenneth Kiyota. Their last names, all beginning with K, would make them my seat companions throughout the next few years. They would make school fun. What I lacked in confidence Sammy and Kenneth had in abundance.

Not long after we were seated, Sammy began to goad me, "Go ask da teacha why her eye all smash." I looked over at our teacher and examined her closely. Miss Yamane's right side looked as if someone had pressed her eye toward the center of her face.

"No," I whispered back. "Go ask her yourself."

"Go ask her, go ask her," Sammy and Kenneth urged, poking me in the arm.

Taking a tiny bit of their confidence, I walked up to the teacher and asked, "How come your eye all smash?" A hush fell over the classroom. I felt courageous for the first time.

The teacher answered, "When I was small, I pulled the cord of the iron when my mother was ironing, and the iron fell on the side of my face. So when your mother is ironing, stay away from the ironing board."

"The cord of the iron" didn't make sense to me because my mother's iron was a cordless gas iron. We had no electricity. I didn't question Miss Yamane's explanation. Instead, I turned around, put both my hands on my hips, looked at the class and proudly announced, "Her face all smash because da iron wen smash her eye." The matter was settled, and the question was never raised again.

I continued to use my newfound confidence and the prodding of the boys. It was a pretty easy thing to do. I asked for crayons to replace our broken ones and walked up to the pencil sharpener. I felt pretty confident until the second day of school, when I would lose it completely and cry for the first time.

"First grade is easy," I thought. I looked at the rows and rows of Aa's, Bb's, Cc's and Dd's that I had carefully written. Like the teacher's sample on the board, my small letters stayed below the dotted middle lines. My capital letters reached the top of the solid lines, and they didn't go over the top dark lines as Sammy's did.

I knew I was getting an A. I could barely wait for my paper to be handed back on the following day.

I could hear my heart beat as Miss Yamane handed me my paper. It would be an A, of course. I saw a big red C written across the page of perfectly written letters.

"What is dis? I want A. I don't want dis mark." I began to sob.

Miss Yamane sighed and explained, "This C is like an A. When you do good work, I put a C on the top. C means corrected. This means good work."

"But I want A," I insisted, using my left sleeve to wipe my eyes and nose.

Being the middle child, I wasn't totally ignorant. I had eavesdropped enough times on my older siblings' conversations to know that A was good and F meant flunk. Where was this A?

And so it began, the education or the un-education of a kindergarten dropout that didn't always bring clarity.

Too many gaps would appear, like a mountain of Swiss cheese. Sammy, on the other hand, was a good teacher.

He taught me how to clean my lunch plate without being forced to eat some of the strange food. "Do this," he said when we took our lunch plates from the cafeteria to the classroom. He scraped off the spinach that he didn't want and dropped it on the ground. We walked close to each other, dropping food between us so that we would not be caught. There were a lot of cries of "Oops" as we spilled our milk on the ground.

He showed me how to leave a tack on the teacher's chair and wear a "poker face" when other students were accused of the crime. Years later, when I was a juror in a rape case and the defense attorney told me, "Your face was the most difficult to read," I thought of Sammy.

I also left my mark as a ghost whisperer with Sammy's help.

I disrupted class one day when I felt a twitch in my shoulder. "A ghost! A ghost! I just felt his hand grab my shoulder!" My dramatic outburst interrupted the quiet reading hour. The teacher dared not scold me because my classmates all knew about Hawaiian ghosts. It would be unthinkable to question their existence. Our village was filled with ghost stories that rose from the old Hawaiian burial grounds. Sammy's mother had told me about a flying hand that came through the window and choked her before going back out the window.

Sammy and Kenneth jumped out of their seats to check my shoulder. "Yeah," Sammy said, "must be from the old Hawaiian graves right outside the window. At night, you can hear the menehunes marching over them with small lights." Years later, I would experience similar twitches in my shoulders and know that they were muscle spasms.

It could have been a coming-of-age time in the fifth- and sixth-grade building had my questions not been flipped aside like pesky flies.

I watched sixth-grader Lani walk up to the teacher with a bloodstain on the back of her skirt. She was quietly sent to the cafeteria.

I turned to whisper to Alice, "Did you see blood on Lani's dress?"

"Yeah, I wonder what happened to her."

"Let's ask the teacher during recess."

As soon as the bell rang, I was at the teacher's desk with my classmates standing behind me.

"What happened to Lani? Is she hurt?"

The teacher lifted her head from the stack of math papers and brusquely said, "Oh, nothing to worry about. She just got her period. When it happens to you, just get a pad and tighten your belt." She dismissed us by returning to her work.

We looked at each other in silence. It was obvious that we all shared the same thoughts.

What? Why must I tighten the belt on my dress? A pad? What am I supposed to do with a pad of paper? Huh?

"Come on," I suggested. "Let's go ask Miss Ota. She's easy to talk to." But we received another brush-off from the cafeteria manager. Miss Ota explained, "When that happens to you, it means you're a woman and you can get pregnant. So be careful."

Not long after this, I snooped into my sister's chest of drawers and found a strange contraption. "Hmmm, what is this? Oh, it must be a belt to help her with her posture."

My sister was often reminded to straighten her shoulders.

During the summer following sixth grade, I found a reddish-brown stain on my panties and tried to bargain with God.

"If you stop this thing, I'll work harder and be good." I tightened the belt on my dress, and soon it went away. But it returned again before summer was over, so I became suspicious of my relationship with God.

I had looked forward to seventh grade because it meant attending Pāhoa High and Intermediate School. I would wear shoes to school and have my first hair permanent.

I wore a new dress sewn by my mother, a lime-green dress with a flared skirt. My hair had been tightly permed in Hilo so that it would last the entire school year. On my feet was a new pair of high wedged sandals, bought from the Variety Shoe Store in Hilo, which gave me a few more inches of height.

I met other seventh graders from Kalapana, ʻOpihikao and Pāhoa. "Hey," Sammy teased, pointing to my tight curls, "You got electrocuted."

At the end of the day, when I stepped off the bus, my brother followed me into the house. He whispered something to my mother. I was quietly led straight into the bedroom and was handed a sanitary napkin and a belt. Why, it was similar to that belt I had found in my sister's chest of drawers. It wasn't for her posture after all.

Only then did I realize that my dress was stained with blood. That meant that when I had gotten off the bus, all the other student riders had seen the back of my dress, just as I had seen Lani's dress in the fifth grade. I had, by then, picked up some information about menstruation from the girls at school. "Did you start your period yet?" was often asked in whispers. We would have to wait until the eighth grade to receive proper information on our sexual development. Until then, we were informed by the coconut wireless.

I became a voracious reader. The newspaper, *Reader's Digest*, movie magazines and the bookmobile were my main sources of information. The bookmobile visited Kapoho once a month, much to my delight.

I was in the eighth grade when one of my questions almost turned into a crisis.

Before the Social Studies teacher could begin his lessons, I raised my hand.

"I have a question," I said. "In yesterday's paper, there was a story of a black man giving blood to a white woman. Does this make the woman black since she now has black blood in her?"

The teacher looked at me in silence for a moment, then said, "Please stay after class. That question is too advanced for this class."

"What?" I wondered. "Did I ask the wrong question?"

When we were alone, he began, "Umm...I couldn't answer your question in class. Black blood doesn't refer to the blood in our bodies. Umm...a person becomes black only after being born of black or part-black parents. In other words," he stumbled, without making eye contact, "it's...umm...through sexual intercourse."

I took the discomfort he showed in saying "sexual intercourse" and made it mine. Without looking at him, I quickly gathered my books and mumbled, "Thank you," and walked out of the classroom.

Three girls waited eagerly outside the door to hear what the teacher had said. I whispered, "It's through sexual intercourse!" We giggled our way to the next class. My giggling stopped later that night when I thought of the teacher. I felt I had passed through another phase in my life, maybe grown up a few notches during that short conference. To have a teacher stumble over my question gave me a sense of power, just as it had when I was six years old and overheard my first-grade teacher tell my mother, "Frances is such a difficult child to understand."

I would ask many more questions in the years to come, but there was one question I never asked. It was shortly after December 7, and I was six years old. "How come dey calling me Jap?"

The Emperor's Kidnapped Daughter

"I'm here by mistake," I announced. "I was born in Emperor Hirohito's family, and somebody kidnapped me and brought me here."

"Say what you like," my father said. He stood there, watching me use an old broomstick to lift a pair of pants from a large pail of water where the rest of his work clothes were soaking overnight. I transferred a pair of his pants into a cracker barrel filled with very hot water almost to the boiling point over an open fire. "Don't burn yourself," he warned. "We don't want the emperor's daughter to get burned."

The mundane process of laundry day was interrupted by my scream, which could be heard at the outhouse a hundred feet away. The broomstick was on the ground, and a fat reddish-green centipede crawled out of a shirt and scurried down the concrete washtub out of sight. Shivers ran down my spine. *Where are the maids? What am I doing, being scared out of my wits by a centipede? This is no life for an emperor's daughter.*

Brown bubbles and steam rose from the clothes. The pungent odor of sugarcane and sweat filled my nostrils.

Bubbles. Ah, champagne bubbles from a crystal-stemmed glass slip down my throat while the sweet fragrance of rose petals fills the air.

"If you don't get educated," my father interrupted, "you'll end up marrying a plantation worker like me, and you'll be doing this for the rest of your life."

"I'm marrying a rich man and will have maids and butlers," I quipped. "When you visit me in my mansion, my butler will show you in. Be sure to wear a suit and tie."

His laughter followed him to the backyard, and I was left in my prison of drudgery.

I turned the homemade wooden washing board onto its flat surface. I lifted a pair of pants steaming at the end of the broomstick and smoothed one leg of the pants flat on the board. Then I rubbed a bar of soap along the length of the pants leg and scrubbed with a hard bristled brush.

Once the pants were scrubbed, I turned the washboard over onto its corrugated side and worked the pants against the board like a baker kneading dough. Pants were rinsed, wrung out and hung on clotheslines under the hot sun. A big load like today's could take half a day.

"The emperor's daughter really has better things to do," I thought, looking down at my hands.

The jagged, broken nails of her red hands become long manicured splashes of crimson color as she walks from one end of the clothesline to the other. Her hands hold a flute instead of wooden clothespins, and the notes from the flute and the trickling of water from a bamboo fountain accompany her through the courtyards of Edo.

On nights when I disregarded my mother's warning to take a bath while it was still light, I sang at the top of my voice to drive away ghosts that might creep into the bathhouse. The kerosene lamp cast strange moving shadows on the wall. I averted my eyes from the window where the faces of ghosts might appear and spoil my song.

"What a beautiful voice." I heard my father's voice interrupt my rendition of "Sentimental Journey." "What a shame to waste such a voice. She belongs in Hollywood."

"Just watch me," I snipped. "Someday I'll be in Hollywood. I'll be riding in a red convertible wearing large sunglasses, with my scarf trailing behind me."

The closest I came to Hollywood was one summer during the sugarcane harvest. Cane was harvested every three years. Every so often, the plantation company changed the regular cane to a different brand that yielded a higher sugar content. This meant that new cane stalks had to be planted between the rows of the old ones. As the new cane stalks began to show their green shoots, the old ones were chopped down. It could take two or three rounds of doing this, working through the entire 13 acres under the hot, sizzling sun.

That summer at nearby Warm Springs, "Hollywood" filmed the movie *Bird of Paradise*, starring Louis Jourdan, Debra Paget and Jeff Chandler. For weeks I stood in the hot cane field and watched the caravans of "Hollywood" pass on the long country road. Sometimes, from the distance, I waved and shouted, "Hey, Louis Jourdan!"—glad that he couldn't see the emperor's daughter dressed in denim jeans and old, faded, long-sleeved work shirts.

It didn't help to hear the neighborhood kids brag, "We went down to Warm Springs today. Jeff Chandler came to talk to us. He's really nice and talked story with us."

I wanted to be with the village children instead of under the hot sun doing slave labor. Kapoho was no place for the emperor's daughter and a future Oscar-winning, Pulitzer Prize-winning poet.

I picked up one of my father's left-handed cane knives. It was sharpened on the opposite side of the blade for left-handed users. Hmmm, the emperor must be left-handed, too. With the sun beating down on my body, I chopped each of the old cane shoots down to the ground.

My sister came over to my row. "You need to chop it down real good so they don't grow back again." She showed me how it was done. Her way would be more time consuming. I couldn't care less about whether they grew again; the sooner I finished, the faster I'd be out of there. Warm Springs and Louis Jourdan's accent were waiting for me. I used my soiled long sleeve to wipe the tears from my face.

Someone had noticed. For the remainder of the summer, whenever I came to the end of a row, the last three feet had already been cut.

Under that hot sun, with sweat sticking my clothes to my body like wet silk and with my muscles aching, lunchtime would be my Hollywood. Every day, it would be like the same script. My oldest brother would peek into the lunch pail and ask, "What do you think we're having for lunch?"

A list of Kapoho cuisine would be shouted out: Spam! Eggs! Vienna sausage! Rice with ume! Tap water in a thermos, champagne for the emperor's daughter.

At the dinner table, after a hard day's work, my father's voice was filled with pride. "Other families hire people to work in their cane fields. We don't need to do that. I'm lucky to have good children."

"Yes, but look at me. I'm stuck in a place that has no electricity or even a water system. We have an outhouse, one battery-run radio, a kerosene stove, not even a pay phone anywhere. We don't even have a car, and Hilo is twenty miles away!"

"I know," my father replied. "I was kidnapped, too." My father's voice faded into the background with the rest of the dinner conversation. Over the sink, doing the dishes later, I belted out one of my favorite songs:

"If I should ever travel, to China I would go,
Japan and South Korea, these lands I'd like to know.

The Philippines I'd visit, the Polynesian isles,
Australia and New Zealand, from pole to pole I'd go.

My home is down Pacific, way down Hawai'i nei,
Oh, may our land be peaceful, forever and for aye.

For now, the reality of being kidnapped in Kapoho closed in. My sister was going to give me my first hair perm. She took a large nail between a pair of metal tongs and held it in the fire under the cracker barrel filled with my father's work clothes. She wound sections of my hair around the hot nail and let them sizzle and burn. There was nothing royal about the smell of burnt hair. That night I awoke from a dream that my hair was straight again. I crawled out from under the futon with a flashlight and found a mirror to check on my perm. I still looked like Bette Davis. I returned to bed and dreamed of seeing myself on movie screens.

In my waking hours, I filled empty shoeboxes with poems, stories, favorite book titles, letters and photos. A pen pal from Michigan sent photos of herself sitting in a tree, munching on a red apple. A pen pal from Maryland sent a picture of herself in a strapless white prom gown in front of a television set in her living room. There was a photo of someone skating on a frozen pond. Letters written on onionskin airmail stationery from a pen pal from France were bundled together with a rubber band. Each letter repeated the last, but he was French, which meant Paris would be my next stop.

A postal worker in a Chicago mailroom sent a letter. "I am handicapped from the war. I work from a wheelchair and suffer from a nervous disorder. I am 34 years old. I work at the post office, and I often see your letters to Michigan pass through my hands. I've always dreamed of Hawaii. Will you write to me?"

"He's too old" was my first thought. I offered to give his name to one of my female teachers. "Don't you want a more matured woman since I'm only a kid?" He rejected the idea.

Then one day, after months of correspondence, he sent a black-and-white photo of himself. How could a man who wrote such beautiful thoughts in blue script not be handsome like William Holden or Robert Taylor? How could a man who began each letter with "My Dear Frances" not be Hollywood-star handsome? I tore up his photo and stopped writing, but I added all his letters to one of my secret boxes. In a box was a story I wrote in fifth grade:

> "Once upon a time, there lived a girl whose classmates were very wealthy. Every September, on the first day of school, they talked about their summer travels to Paris, New York City and London. The girl listened in envy. The following summer while her friends traveled to all those faraway places, she spent her summer in the public library. When she returned to school in September, she told stories about her travels to Africa, India and Russia. She described each country, her favorite

places and their people. She repeated a conversation between a Communist and herself in Moscow. No one ever discovered she had never left home."

Determined to fit in at those elegant cocktail parties in New York, Paris and London, the emperor's daughter reads Good Housekeeping, Vogue *and the latest Sears catalog. She keeps up with* Time *magazine's Ten Best Fiction and Nonfiction Books. She studies* The New Yorker's *cartoons and subscribes to* Psychology Today. *She is still using the outhouse but is ready to discuss any book or current event, with a glass of wine held in a hand bedecked with diamond bracelets and rings.*

Later, as a freshman in college, I was working as a live-in maid for room and board when earthquakes and lava flows slowly demolished Kapoho. I was studying for exams. The villagers evacuated with the help of the Red Cross and the National Guard. No one knew about Emperor Hirohito's daughter. My shoeboxes were left behind. ▣

Twenty-Seven Minus Nine

"Eh, Sammy. You ever wonder how those rich Honolulu kids figure out their arithmetic?"

"What do you mean?"

"Look at this. Twenty-seven minus nine. If we had shoes, we would never figure this out."

"Maybe rich kids are smarter than us. I bet their parents buy them fancy math stuff."

It was a good thing Sammy and I had last names beginning with K. I would never have passed Arithmetic had we not sat together to share our bare toes. How else could I have subtracted anything from a number greater than twenty when I had only ten fingers and ten toes?

Napua, whose last name also began with K, sat behind me, and I didn't need to turn around to know she was there; I could smell her. Twice the size of me, she wore her thick black hair in two braids, slicked and drenched in coconut oil. She was not interested in my bare toes, only in my grades. She stretched her neck to see the grades on my assignments each time they were returned. Having done her snooping all during September since school started, she waited until October to give me an assignment of her own.

"Eh, do all my math homework or I goin' put kahuna on you." She showed me her fist.

By the third grade I had a full, inaccurate, child's understanding of the power of the Hawaiian priest, the kahuna. I'd eavesdropped on enough village stories to know that the kahuna was no one to be trifled with.

"The doctor can't figure out why he's sick. I think the kahuna put a curse on him."

"You better not piss around Hawaiian graves. The kahuna will get you."

"Hawaiians know how to put the kahuna on you."

Napua was Hawaiian, so every night I wrote two sets of math homework. There was simply no way to avoid Napua. Each time an assignment was given, I felt her eyes burning on me, compelling me to look at her. She held her clenched fist close to her chest, and she mouthed, "Kahuna."

"Should I tell Sammy," I wondered, "since he's Hawaiian and maybe he can ward off her curse?" No, I had promised Napua I wouldn't tell anyone, and she might put the kahuna on him and we'd both be in trouble.

I hated her. She left a painful ache inside me whenever I thought of school. I wished she'd flunk out and quit school. I was also scared of her, so I did her homework for the next two years before my wish came true. Napua remained in sixth grade until age 16, the legal age to drop out of school. It will always remain a mystery why she dropped me as her mathematician after the fourth grade. By then, I was solving bigger problems with Sammy.

"Eh, Sammy," I said, lying on my back, looking up at the sky. "Did you see Charlie Chaplin last night?"

"No, I'm goin' this Saturday to see *The Lone Ranger.*"

"Charlie Chaplin was funny. He was so hungry, he boiled his shoes to make soup. He ate his shoelace like spaghetti. They keep showing the same war news."

I watched the clouds, white chiffon gowns of the wind, swaying against the clear blue sky, wedding gowns, lacy veils and silk trains, flowing and moving like brides down the aisles. An ache of unknown source filled me to the brim. Sammy saw the faces of Churchill and the Lone Ranger.

"Eh, Sammy, I bet if Truman and Stalin got on their backs like this and looked at the clouds and the skies, they would think of peace, not war."

"Yeah, this is better than sitting around a round table, that's for sure. Hard to make war when you look up the sky."

"Yeah, a peace conference outside in the fields. All the leaders on their backs like this, looking up at the clouds and feeling the wind on their faces. For sure, they wouldn't make war."

"And they shouldn't wear shoes."

"Yeah, and they better not have toe jam." We lay there laughing, wriggling our toes in the air, far removed from the war news.

Eventually we did wear shoes when we entered the seventh grade and were bused to Pāhoa High and Intermediate School. After years of climbing trees, sliding down hillsides on cardboard boxes and walking through cane fields looking for sweet stalks of cane in bare feet, to suddenly stuff our feet into shoes took its toll. Every morning, I covered my blistered feet with Band-Aids before painfully slipping them into my shoes. At the end of the school day, there was such relief getting those damn shoes off my feet.

It became obvious that no one heard Sammy's and my idea of the "Open-Air Peace Conference." War clouds with different names continued to float past us throughout the years.

I became the Tokyo Rose of the Korean War. I volunteered passionate reports of the war to anyone who'd listen. My hero worship of General MacArthur, with his pipe clenched in his mouth, turned me into the Ernie Pyle of World War II. I wrote poems filled with rage, lashing out at President Truman for firing my war hero at the 38th Parallel. MacArthur's "Old soldiers never die, they only fade away" played in my head like an old song.

No matter. MacArthur's face with his pipe and hat plastered my notebook pages; his square-jawed Dick Tracy profile became my favorite pastime doodle. Patrick Henry's "Give me liberty or give me death" speech rolled off my tongue. I was emotionally immersed in war and patriotism. The boys in school thought of a new nickname for me.

"Hey, Ko-li-ahn Tabi," they called me, referring to Korean tabi, or socks, because of my obsessions.

Fortunately, Sammy's passion for fun diluted my obsession with the war. Our family extended into his, and we spent summers and weekends camping out at the beach and celebrated Christmases and other holidays together. We bodysurfed in the rough waves and threw out lines to catch shoreline fishes. I drank a lot of the ocean during those years with Sammy playing monster eel.

During my senior year in high school, my dreams seemed a grasp away. Sammy reminded me of this one day near graduation.

"Eh, congratulations. I heard you got two scholarships to the University of Hawai'i. That was a nice picture in the newspaper. Some smart, you."

"Not really, Sammy. I wrote an essay on why I wanted to go to college and sent it to UH alumni. I didn't show it to anyone, not even you. I figured I had no chance compared to all those Hilo kids, and how shame if I didn't get it. So I kept it a secret. Mrs. Lau got really mad because the scholarship committee told her my paper was poorly written, but they liked the content. She scolded me and said my poor writing insulted her because she was my English teacher. She made it a big deal."

Sammy interrupted, "You should have told her, 'Eh, next time teach me good so I won't embarrass you with my writing.'"

"Eh, Sammy, maybe I shouldn't wear shoes to college."

Before we graduated from high school, Sammy and I made a pact. "Sammy, promise me something. If I can't find one of those English professors to marry me, promise you'll marry me. I don't want to be an old maid. So shame if nobody marries me."

"You're goin' college, I'm goin' drive a bulldozer. No, I don't think you want to marry me. Go find that English professor, since you like to read."

Where would I ever find such a creature? "No, Sammy, let's make a pact. If by age thirty I'm not married, promise to marry me."

"Okay, it's a deal."

Forty-five years after we had made that deal, I stood in his living room and watched him walk in.

"Oh, Sammy," I said silently, holding back my tears. "Oh, Sammy." He had braces on his broomstick legs and arms and negotiated the short distance with the help of a walker. His daughter held him up from the back. She led him to a bed in the living room and helped him sit on a waterproof pad. Despite his wreck of a body, I saw traces of Sammy.

"Sammy, I'm Hideko," I prompted. His eyes lit up, and his whole face broke into a smile. I kissed him on the cheek and sat next to him.

"Sammy, I'm still single. Guess what, I found out English professors are as dull as the back of a cane knife. Remember your promise to marry me?" The smile in his eyes and his nod told me he remembered. "I came to collect on that promise." His body shook with silent laughter.

He kept his eyes on me as I chatted about old times. "You still look rascal and handsome," I said. I rubbed his back. The feeling of affection for my old friend overwhelmed me. I looked down at Sammy's orthopedic shoes. My feet were bare.

I'm back in third grade. "Twenty-seven minus nine. Eh, Sammy, I need your toes for this one." He moves his two bare feet toward me. I add seven of his toes to my twenty fingers and toes and subtract nine. "Answer's eighteen."

"Sammy, remember how we used to borrow each other's toes and fingers to do math in Miss Nakamura's class?" He nodded and smiled. "Quick, what's thirty-two minus nine?" Playfully, Sammy reached down to untie his shoes. Silent and loud laughter burst from both of us at the same time.

"Guess what, Sammy? After all these years, I still can't balance my checkbook. I don't have enough fingers and toes."

His face lit with laughter, and I saw the Sammy I remembered. After 15 minutes, he looked tired, and I had run out of things to say; it was time to leave.

Sammy had a stroke 11 years ago. I wanted to hear his voice. I wanted to know what he was thinking and feeling. I felt sadness wrap around me, choking me. I wanted...but it was time to go. I stood up to leave. His hand was on the gift and note I had given him.

Sammy, I will always treasure our childhood.
Love, Hideko

He followed me with his eyes as I walked to the door. I paused, turned to look at him and said, "Sammy, the next time I come, I'm giving you a bath." ▩

You Are Going to Hell

I was eight years old, walking home alone from school on a narrow three-mile dirt road, swinging my homemade schoolbag against my leg. I hardly noticed the heavy forest of mango and guava trees around me. I kept close to the edge, though cars seldom traveled this way. I didn't notice the tall, dark figure approaching from the opposite direction until he was a few yards away. His black coat flapped in the wind as he hurried toward me. I inched closer to the side to let the shadow pass.

He stopped, his eyes staring at me from beneath the wide brim of his black hat. His head moved from side to side, and I heard him say, "Oh, my poor child, you are going to hell. I don't see you in Catechism, so I know you're not Catholic. Only Catholics go to heaven."

Frightened and confused, I rubbed an imaginary smudge of dirt off my dress. From the look of sympathy on his face, I was not doing something right. My family was not doing something right. Right was being Catholic, and we were Buddhists. Shaking his head, he hurried away, echoing his curse to my back, "You are going to hell, my child." I ran home as fast as I could. My encounter with the priest was added to my shoebox of secrets.

Once a week, on Wednesday afternoons, the Catholic children were released an hour early to attend Catechism.

"I wish I were Catholic like them," I thought as I watched them file out of the room. "So lucky to have early release from class and not have to do extra reading work." Some of them goaded us, saying, "Too bad you're not Catholic. You can't get free time off."

We had a Buddhist shrine at home, and my mother regularly burned incense and prayed her Buddhist sutras. These familiar rituals were repeated in Sunday school, which I attended until I was 18.

When I was 15, the entire Buddhist community joined in the excitement caused by the visit of the Buddhist abbot from Japan. Rites were performed to initiate children into Buddhism.

"The Kakugawa children are the only ones not being baptized," I argued with my father. My father, who walked miles to the beach to fish for food, simply said, "Going to church is like going to the beach. There are many ways to find the beach. Wait until you're grown up to choose your own way."

My father attended church only for weddings and funerals. Otherwise, the ocean was all the church he seemed to need. Religion, like other family values, was placed on the table like a buffet, offering us our own choices.

Still, I was impressionable then, and vulnerable and even romantic. The declaration from the priest that afternoon continued to echo behind me for a long time. It became a voice of authority in religious matters, above the teachings of Buddha in Sunday school. It was impossible to not notice Billy Graham and the Pope on magazine covers. I devoured articles on Billy Graham and placed him on my hero list. Being like everyone else in the outside world meant believing in God instead of Buddha; this I knew, for nowhere did I see the face of Buddha in *Look* or *Life* magazines. I also knew that hell was a fiery place with Satan in red, waiting for sinners. We memorized the Lord's Prayer in school and even sang "Jesus Loves Me" during music period; our curriculum was as open-ended as religion in my home.

The priest in my box of secrets would nag me until the day a neighbor made me an offer I couldn't refuse. Finally, I could find a way to dilute that curse given by the priest.

After school and on weekends, I cleaned and boxed tomatoes for Mr. Uyeki, a part-time farmer. One Christmas, Mr. Uyeki said, "You work very hard, so I buy you anything you want."

I thought of my hours cleaning 50-pound crates of tomatoes, dipping rags in pails of water with maggots floating in them, the unsuccessful scrubbing of my hands after work to get rid of the smell. Yes, I had earned Mr. Uyeki's gift.

"A necklace," I said, without hesitation. "I want a cross on a chain."

Mr. Uyeki was a staunch Buddhist, and I was surprised that he didn't question my wish. He bought me exactly what I'd asked for. I proudly showed the necklace to a Catholic classmate. She looked at it and quipped, "It won't protect you unless it gets blessed by the priest." I handed the cross over to her with instructions to be sure that it got blessed properly. When she returned it a few days later, did it shine a little brighter? I was certain it did. Perhaps now my journey to hell could somehow be avoided. I put it safely in the bottom of my chest of drawers for safekeeping. Unlike Catholic children, who wore their crosses around their necks, I kept mine hidden.

During my senior year in high school, I taught Sunday school whenever the Buddhist minister was unable to make the trip from the church in

Keaāu. I didn't use any prescribed Buddhist texts for my sermons. They were boring, stale stories of Buddha's young life, told and retold by every minister who taught Sunday school. English was the ministers' second language, so we wandered off into our minds as they minced their sermons into unrecognizable language. Instead, I chose stories I found in *Our Romance, Good Housekeeping* and *Reader's Digest*. I ended each story with a Buddhist lesson. I rewrote endings when necessary, to fashion characters into persons who performed acts of kindness and compassion. "This is being Buddhist" was the moral of each story. My cross stayed in the drawer.

After I turned 18 and graduated from high school, I left Kapoho for the first time and stepped into a haole world that I was completely unprepared for. I began my freshman year in college, working as a live-in maid for the Evanses, a family of five. I got room and board and $25 a month.

I lived in a house that had electricity and indoor plumbing; I had my own room and a bed. In Kapoho, we had outhouses and chopsticks and one fork.

That one fork turned us into haoles around the dinner table. My father found a fork along the railroad tracks, and it caused quite a stir at dinnertime.

"I want the fork! I want the fork!" led to five kids taking turns with the fork.

Here, I was expected to set a table for breakfast and dinner using flatware settings with names and functions I could barely guess. Each evening I stood for a moment at the dining room table, like someone in deep meditation, conjuring an image of what went where: forks on the left, spoons on the right. The parade of plates and glasses and silverware seemed endless.

"Life is too hard," I wrote in an essay. "I should show them how to eat with chopsticks!"

One afternoon, Mrs. Evans made a pot of stew in the pressure cooker and asked me to set the table. I did so, with soup spoons.

"Oh, Frannie," Mrs. Evans said. "You must not have heard me; we're having stew tonight." She quickly replaced the spoons with forks, without a trace of finding fault.

I had heard her right. At home, "Hawaiian stew" was more soup and meat and vegetables, poured over scoops of rice. Spoons did nicely there, but not here.

"What?" I thought, watching her ladle the thick gravy with meat and vegetables onto the plates. "This is called stew? Where's the rice?"

As for rice, I brought Kapoho into the Evanses' kitchen. When first asked to cook rice, I calculated what a family of six would need by Kapoho standards. At home, I cooked five cups of rice for our family of seven, which filled our bowls and bellies for a single meal and left enough for the next day's lunch. But when I saw Mrs. Evans serve a few spoonfuls on our plates, I started to catch on that our staple was their side dish. It was the first and last time we had rice pudding that lasted a week.

I may as well have been in the devil's workshop. Modern appliances escaped me completely. I was babysitting one evening while the parents went to a movie. The girls knocked a lamp over, and I stood petrified, watching the thing spark and sputter as it hit the floor. I looked at the snake-like cord running menacingly into the wall and was afraid of being electrocuted. I called the theater and left a message. The Evanses' names were flashed onto the screen, so Mrs. Evans went to the box office to call home and instructed me to unplug the lamp. She thanked me for calling her. I learned to think, "Unplug first, call later, stupid."

Everyday routines were familiar enough: preparing lunches and dinners, doing laundry, dressing the children and making the beds. But it was a shock to learn what a bumpkin I really was, the gaps in my experience that Kapoho simply did not fill. To make matters worse, I was a Japanese domestic serving a haole family. I reminded myself, "You need to do this to get a college education. Forget this shame of being a maid, and pretend you're in prison for the next four years. Four years of hell will be over before you know it." I managed to cut that sentence down to three and a half years for my Bachelor of Education degree.

When I was first interviewed to be the Evanses' maid, Mrs. Evans made it clear that my dignity would be preserved: "You are part of our family. The children are not to call you a maid." Every day, one child was designated "Child of the Day," and she had the privilege of sitting on the front seat of the car with me when Mr. or Mrs. Evans transported us to and from our schools. The "Child of the Day" had dinner with me in the kitchen while the rest of the family ate in the dining room. It was a privilege for the three girls, but for me, it was a magical transformation from being just a maid to becoming the maid of honor. The three girls' affection toward me and Mrs. Evans's wisdom helped to blur the imprint of "maid" on my name.

"Oh, is that your maid?" one of their visiting playmates asked one day, and Debbie, the five-year-old, answered, "Oh, no, that's Frannie." I also became the girls' confidante and listened to their complaints about "being the oldest and always being blamed" or "being bossed around by my two older sisters." I was there when one of the litters of pups was born, and seven-year-old Nicki rushed to me and explained, "Frannie, I thought pups came out of the mouth, but guess what, they come from here!" And she pointed to her private parts.

On my last day as maid, I was waiting for the bus when Nicki ran into her room and returned with her most treasured crystal bird and said, "Here, Frannie, I want you to have this." I learned to receive gifts from a child that day, and I still have that bird.

Mrs. Evans, a tall and vivacious woman, wore sadness in her eyes, like the springer spaniels she raised in the backyard. One day, she stood by the window and said, as though she were thinking aloud, "Frannie, never marry the oldest son." I didn't need an explanation, because family functions were centered around Mr. Evans's needs and pleasure. Monday nights were movie nights, and even a sick child would not change that.

I carried my clothes in paper bags when I went home on certain weekends. A week before my first exams, Mrs. Evans bought me a leather overnight bag. "We're celebrating your first finals," she said.

After my family had been evacuated from Kapoho during an eruption, Mrs. Evans brought out a complete set of fine china, saying, "Frannie, I've had this set for so long, and it's been cluttering up our cupboards for years. I hope your family will help me get this off my hands." My mother had fine china for the first time. Mr. Evans offered my father a night watchman's job at his business. I didn't take his offer home.

My monthly $25 wage was hidden under a dish by the kitchen door. The children were not to know I was a hired member of the family, so on payday, Mrs. Evans used her head and eyes to signal me that my money was under the dish by the door.

My awkwardness and lack of confidence took center stage at the Evanses' formal sit-down dinners. I felt invisible in people's presence by not being acknowledged at all; I was the maid. At one of these dinners, I spilled gravy on the tablecloth where Mrs. Fulton sat. She immediately used her napkin to sop up the spill, then gave it to me and said, "Please get me another napkin." I took her soiled napkin back to the kitchen, but I couldn't find a matching napkin, no matter how frantically I rummaged through the drawer, determined to find something that I knew wasn't there. All the napkins were being used. I was standing there panic-stricken when Mrs. Evans came through the swinging door with her napkin in her hand.

"Frannie," she said, "I know we're out of napkins. Watch this." I watched her shake her napkin out and carefully refold it. "A word of advice," she said. "Never use your own napkin—keep it clean for occasions like this." She winked at me and said, "Here, give this to Mrs. Fulton." She followed me out with a pitcher of water.

I was learning fast. On Christmas Eve, a car came up the driveway, and a woman got out carrying a Christmas gift. "Damn," Mrs. Evans whispered, "I didn't expect anything from the Carlsons." I took a poinsettia plant off the kitchen counter, rearranged the red bow around the pot and handed it to her. The look of surprise on her face told me that we were finally in cahoots and that I was brilliant.

She took the flowers and greeted the visitor,

"Hi! I was just about to drive over to your place. Merry Christmas!" She returned to the kitchen with the Carlsons' gift. She chuckled, "The secret in life, Frannie, is always keep a spare."

"Always keep a spare" later played in my head like a tape when I read "The Sleeping Beauty" to the girls at bedtime. If Sleeping Beauty's mother, the queen, had been as wise as Mrs. Evans, that fairy tale would have had a faster "happily ever after" ending. As the story went, the queen had only 12 dinner dishes, and there were 13 fairies in the kingdom. So one of the fairies was not invited. It was that fairy who cast a death spell on the princess, and the last of the 12 fairies was only able to lessen the curse with a hundred-year sleep. Always keep a spare.

Our routine was broken one summer with the arrival of the children's cousin from California. Ruthie was Catholic, her parents were divorced and she came with a bundle of problems. One day she confided, "There are two people who love me in this world. You and me. After I leave, I'll be the only one who loves me."

"No, there's one more person who loves you all the time." Her face rearranged itself as if she were trying to fit in a missing piece in a puzzle.

"Who?" she asked. "When I leave here, I'll be all alone. No one loves me except you and me."

"God," I said. "God loves you all the time, especially when you're feeling sad and alone." The moment I said, "God," I thought of the cross.

The next day, I took the cross out of my dresser and handed it to her. "Ruthie," I said, "this cross is to remind you that God is always with you and He loves you."

She was delighted, caressed the cross, put it around her neck and said, "Now there are three people who love me." During the rest of her visit, the cross was always visible and remained her constant companion. She was eight years old.

I watched her leave at the airport, the cross glinting across the tarmac, and I saw in her lightened steps that she had a friend who would be with her as a loving companion instead of uncertain shadows. The cross had finally come to rest in the right hands.

My relationship with the Evanses continued throughout the years. The entire family went to the airport when I left to attend the Mānoa campus on O'ahu. The girls were even flown to O'ahu to have dinners with me until they were able to adjust to the new maid who had replaced me. They celebrated my college graduation, and Mrs. Evans and I exchanged Christmas cards until 2009. I was able to share this story with her, much to her delight.

The Chisel: A Kapoho Story

"Look at that stupid man! He's kissing Kapoho! He might as well kiss my ass!" Keoni's young voice bursts out of him as he watches an old man struggle out of a taxi and stretch his arms toward the sky as if to hold everything that he sees. He lets out a loud "Ahhh" and drops to his knees to kiss the ground. Still on his knees, he takes a white handkerchief out of his pocket and wipes the tears flowing down his face. "How can anyone love this place so much? There's no electricity, no television, only stinking outhouses! He must be crazy!" Keoni shouts in disbelief.

Slowly Keoni's eyes cleared. There was no man now. There was no Kapoho. The outhouses were gone, too. Kapoho was extinct under megatons of lava. Keoni stood next to his rental car, a brand-new Mercedes.

Keoni wasn't kissing any old Kapoho, that was for sure. In fact, it wasn't by choice that he was back. He should have taken care of this business of getting rid of the property years ago. His father had always said to Keoni when he didn't come in to dinner after the first call, "Haole talk, one time 'nuff." He had meant to sell the property but had never gotten around to it, and time was running out.

Keoni looked around, even with nothing at all to see but an endless field of dead rock with an occasional coconut or mango tree. He bent over to pick up a piece of lava rock and saw a piece of paper stuck between the rocks.

"Maybe it's one of my poems," he thought, feeling foolish for even thinking of his poems. It was just a piece of old newspaper. The memory of his first published poem jostled loose a long-forgotten memory. It was the day he had put away his dream of becoming a writer.

Charlie runs and huffs up the road to the porch where Keoni and Sammy sit huddled around a battery-run Philco radio, listening to the Yankees and Dodgers game. There is more static than the announcer's voice.

"Eh, Keoni, I heard they wen print your poem in one magazine."

Keoni takes a dollar of out his pocket, holds it with two fingers as though it were a piece of trash and says, "Look, Charlie, big deal, I got only a dollar for it."

Sammy looks at the dollar. "But Keoni, you want to be one writer. So what if you wen get only one dollar? That proves you one writer already. That's good, man."

Keoni shakes his head. "What can you get for a dollar, Sammy? Eh, haole style, that's not where the money is." He shoved the dollar back into his pocket.

"Christ!" Keoni thought. "That was fifty years ago!" He looked around. There was nothing at all now, only dead rock among some isolated coconut and papaya trees, the remains of a lava flow that had buried most of his village. No man with a handkerchief, no smart-mouthed boy. Just dead rock in every direction. Nothing had changed since that day. Nothing would ever change. He brushed a fly off his sleeve and looked down at his three-piece suit. "It cost a bundle," he thought, but then, all of his clothes were expensive. Well, one thing had changed: that smart-mouthed barefoot kid was gone for good, along with the rest of Kapoho.

Keoni looked up and surveyed his property with the sweep of his eyes. Everything else was frozen in time. Just one big pile of worthless rock left to him by his father. Keoni didn't hold it against him. It was all the old man had had to leave him. It had been worthless then, and it was worthless now. He had to get rid of it, and quickly. He would have to sell it below market price to get the job done. Time was running out.

The place was silent except for the voices in his head. "I'm too busy for this crap," he complained to himself, but the voices got louder, and with the voices came images.

"Back off, you old pirate! This treasure's mine!" Two boys circle each other, sword in hand, long sticks pulled through the ends of rubber zoris, a perfect hilt for a sword. Blade against blade! Click! Crack! They fight until one falls dead on the ground and the other stands victoriously over him, with the tip of his blade against the dead man's chest.

How long had it been since King Arthur, Blackbeard and Errol Flynn had inhabited his body? How long since he'd played with his friends?

"Let's test 'em out. Race you to the post office!" Sardine cans press against their feet as they grip tightly on the rope threaded through the cans and hobble off toward the Kapoho Post Office.

"Dis betta den walking on lava rock!" Charlie shouts.

"Hey," Keoni yells back, "we could patent this and get rich!" They laugh so hard that they roll over on their backs and don't make it to the end of the race.

That was the first time he'd seriously thought about how to get out of Kapoho. Two measures of "Hey Jude" interrupted his reverie. He reached into his pocket and turned his cell phone off. He thought of two old cans of pork and beans.

"Can you hear me now?" he shouts to Charlie over their walkie-talkie made

from the two empty cans connected by a piece of string.

"Can you hear me now?" Charlie mimics. "Man, Keoni, you tink you haole? Can you hear me now? Yeah, stupid, you getting so close, I can smell da fish you wen eat for lunch!"

"One time 'nuff," Keoni mumbled as he stepped onto the flow that was left of his boyhood. He walked toward a mango tree on the mauka side of the lot that marked the separation of his property from the neighbor's. He had carved his name on this tree with his first pocket knife. Was his name still there? He knelt down and trailed his fingers over the bark. Yes, "Keoni" was still there, barely felt under his fingers.

He continued walking around the property, looking for the surveyor's boundary lines. He had made a promise to himself as he watched his father working long hours as a cane cutter. "Someday, I'm going to live in big cities where skyscrapers tower over trees, where neon lights turn night into day, where money falls out of my pockets and I can afford anything and anyone I want." Even then, he had known instinctively that he had to clean up his pidgin if he were to get out of that place. And he did. Not only did skyscrapers surround him, but he had his office in an upper floor of one. He was a success, and his children were in the best of private schools.

He wandered around the lot, and more memories found their way in, like that lava flow toward Kapoho when he was a kid.

"Pee-cue! Pee-cue!" Keoni hears the sound of ricocheting bullets against the rocks as he aims his finger at the sheriff and misses. "Pee-cue! Pee-cue!" He feels the sudden imaginary jolt of pain and slowly falls to the ground, holding onto his chest, covering his bullet wound.

The sheriff pulls down the red kerchief covering Keoni's nose and mouth. "Where's the holdup money from the stagecoach?"

Keoni looks at the sheriff, opens his mouth and struggles, "I…I…I…," then drops his head down and dies.

"Pee-cue! Pee-cue!" Keoni muttered as he walked on the property, still looking for boundary markings. Did kids nowadays play cowboys and robbers? The property was worthless, but he had to get rid of it. He came to a slight depression in the ground and stopped. "That must be where the koi pond was, next to the house," he thought, "and the outhouse must have been over there." He thought of his sister. The outhouse had been her favorite place of refuge. He had told her once, "You are so weird, someday when I become a famous writer I'm going to write about you in the outhouse."

He winced as he remembered her reply: "If you no stop peeking on me, you not goin' live long enough to be a writa."

The survey was over. He sat on an old tree stump, staring at the hills where he had slid down so many times on cardboard boxes, imagining he was sledding over snow-covered hills. So many things had slid from his life since then; his wife had left him, and his children called him only when they wanted a down payment for a new car or needed extra cash for some electronic gadget. He hardly saw them anymore.

Keoni stared at where there once was a bamboo grove.

His father gauges a few bamboo poles with his hands until he finds just the one he wants. He slices the bamboo into strips, soaks the strips in warm water, bends them to make a diamond form and ties them together with thread. He carefully lays the bamboo on newspaper to cut the newspaper to the shape of the diamond, and using mashed cooked rice, he pastes the bamboo onto the paper. He finishes by tying a long string to the narrow end of the diamond and pastes on bows made from travel ads to complete the tail.

"Come, Keoni," he says. "We go fly your kite."

"That's a kite?" It's too homemade for a boy from Kapoho. It looks nothing like the one he saw in the Sears catalog. Oh, but how that kite flies! He can feel the strong pull of the kite in the wind as he runs with it, soaring above the mango trees. Kites, birds, airplanes, they always capture Keoni's imagination. He imagines himself as a passenger on an airplane, watching his tiny island grow smaller and smaller through the window.

Keoni's mouth began to water as he ran his tongue over his lips. He spent so many years learning to hate rice. Exhausted, he tried to stop these thoughts, but like his stock market deals, he couldn't close them off.

"I want a horse like Trigga." That nagging whine turned his thoughts to one particular Christmas morning.

He is the first to go to the Christmas tree, a pine tree covered with paper chains and bells made from last year's Christmas wrap. On the top, a star, covered with gold wrapping paper. He finds a present under the tree with his name on it. It's wrapped in the comic section of the newspaper. He tears the wrapping off and finds a hobby horse inside, carved from koa wood. Keoni looks at his father. "I wanted a real horse," he says, and he leaves the hobby horse under the tree after all the presents are opened.

"Damn," Keoni thought, kicking his foot into the ground. "Where is that horse? It must be in the crate of belongings Mom gave me after Dad died." His father's toolbag with his old chisel was there. Keoni had put it into storage, intending to deal with it later.

Keoni wrapped his arms around himself as if he were cold. "Damn, these memories."

Keoni observes his father from the doorway. His father has his head down, working next to a dimly lit kerosene lamp. Keoni wants to say something, but he knows he shouldn't bother his father. He watches his father's hands, cracked and callused like old leather, chisel away at a piece of wood. His father lays the chisel and mallet on the workbench and grabs a sheet of sandpaper. Keoni walks over to the workbench and picks up the chisel. The burnished handle is still warm from his father's grip. He feels the balance of the old chisel in his hand. Keoni senses his father looking over at him. Keoni waits, but his father says nothing. Keoni lays the chisel back on the workbench and walks away.

Keoni's eyes moistened. He thought of his own children, John and Jenni. "What memories do they have of me? I give them everything they want. But everything I give comes from credit cards." He didn't like the thought, but it was too late to undo the past.

On his way to his car, he paused to take one last look at where the old house had once stood, next to the tree with his carved name. He bent over and scooped up a handful of dirt and pressed it to his mouth. He brushed off his pants, and with the taste of Kapoho still on his lips, he slowly drove out. He would not be returning again. Above the sound of tires rumbling over the loose rocks, he heard a boy's voice, *"I'm out of here, Kapoho, and you can kiss my ass!"* He looked in the rear-view mirror and saw a young Keoni giving the finger to his village. Keoni pressed a little harder on the accelerator and drove off.

"Look at this, Jenni." John held up a bunch of tattered notebooks and flipped through the pages. "I didn't know he wrote poems."

"I think he wanted to be a writer," Jenni replied. "He mentioned it once when I was working on a poetry assignment in high school. It sounded like some dream he had when he was a kid. He said something about giving it up for a dollar."

"Glad he did. You can't eat poetry." John pulled a folder out and leafed through it. "What's this? This looks like the deed to the Kapoho property. I thought he sold that years ago."

"I thought so, too. I know he went back there a couple of times."

"Now here's something strange. A chisel. Why would he keep this in his bank box? It's just an old chisel."

"Grandpa used to do a lot of woodcarving. Maybe it was his."

"This is weird. Where's the rest of his papers? He had lots of assets, but there's nothing here. I can't believe it, Jenni. We need to get in touch with his lawyer."

"I'll give her a call. What should we do with all this stuff? Dump it?"

"I'll take the deed. Maybe we can find a sucker stupid and crazy enough to want a piece of Kapoho. Let's leave the rest in the box for now. We can get rid of it later after the funeral." They returned the items to the deposit box and left the bank.

No one really knew Keoni very well, but a lot of people knew him. They all came to his funeral and did their best to give him an aloha send-off, haole style. After the last person left, the funeral director walked to the casket to close it. He stood there puzzled for a moment. He saw a bunch of notebooks on the deceased's chest and in his hands, an old carpenter's chisel. He slowly put the lid down. ▣

It Was Once Upon a Time

"I raised myself" flew out of my mouth more than once after I became the all-knowing college graduate. No one disputed me.

"Say whatever you like," my mother responded. So I did. It was easy to come to this conclusion from all the books I had buried my face in since the day I learned to read.

Parents in novels weren't anything like my own. They conversed with their children at the dinner table, shared the day's events and asked, "How was your day, dear?" They lectured about what was right and wrong and regulated house rules and curfews. Fathers had one-on-one conversations with their daughters about career dreams, while mothers explained the facts of life. They gave weekly allowances, paid their children for chores and went on vacations together. More importantly, parents talked to their children in long paragraphs. That was the true American family. I knew that as a kid. I read about them.

My father was a laborer, a cane cutter working in the fields from dawn to dusk. He spent his evening walking miles to go fishing to put fish on our dinner table.

He often awakened us in the middle of the night. "Wake up, wake up, come and eat mullet. Better to eat fresh." We sat around the dinner table, half asleep, eating slices of raw mullet soaked in shoyu, hot mustard and lemon juice. You didn't see this in movies or in books.

Day after day, my mother sat hunched over her sewing machine, pumping the pedal, making clothes for the villagers. Most of her conversations were with clients who came with Sears and Montgomery Ward catalogs in hand, wanting a replica of the latest fashion. "Stand still. If I measure wrong, you get crooked pants," I often heard from the porch.

After my mother was diagnosed with Alzheimer's, I began to think about my family life. What I found was a silhouette without a face. I was never really there; I was daydreaming, designing life somewhere else, in New York City or Hollywood. As I watched my mother's dying face, I wondered how two parents, with third- and fifth-grade educations, could have started their family as strangers in an arranged marriage and raised five children without the help of

Dr. Spock. They taught me without lessons or lectures, and I learned without knowing I was learning. They told stories from their own childhood, from the folklore and myths of their grandparents. Without knowing it, these became the conversations I never had. But I never knew that as a child.

My father, the oldest child, was forced to drop out of third grade to help his mother care for his five younger siblings.

"I had to run over ten miles to go to the store while other children were in school. All I remember are scoldings from my mother; I could never please her. But my stepfather was a nice man."

Years later, when I returned to his bedside as he lay dying from stomach cancer, I saw him as a barefoot nine-year-old boy running long, hot miles on a gravel road to appease his mother, and I wept more for that little boy than for the man who was dying.

I wept for my mother, too. My fingers instinctively curled, as if to grasp a magic wand to return my mother to her youth and to the capture of something she never had. "You are lucky," she often told her granddaughters. "Grandma never dated and went out with boys. Grandma couldn't choose her own husband. In our days, it was all arranged."

My mother brought to parenting her own manual of child rearing. Spankings were unknown to us, as were reprimands. My sister and brothers and I slept in one room on futons spread out on the floor. We talked late into the night, rehashing a Charlie Chaplin movie or mercilessly impersonating our principal, Mrs. James. Our giggles and laughter bounced off the walls until we heard my father, from the next room, clear his throat. We knew it was a signal to shut up and go to sleep, and we did.

When I wanted cash for candy, or a box of sanitary napkins, my mother's handbag was in the top drawer of her bureau. I took what I needed and told her in passing, "I took some money." Other kids used allowances, and I envied them. Why couldn't I have parents who were more American?

There was an understanding that whatever chores were mine, I would grow into them or they would grow into me. When I was six, I observed my oldest brother building a fire under a wooden tub.

"What you doing?" I asked.

"Making furo fire," he said to my back as I skipped off to some new distraction.

When I was 12, I hunched on my knees and watched intently as he poured kerosene onto the ashes in the fireplace under the wooden bathtub. Two pieces of firewood were laid about a foot apart on the ashes. Two more were put crosswise on top, and he didn't stop until the pyramid reached almost to the top of the fireplace. He lit a match and threw it on the ashes drenched with kerosene. The fire whooshed and engulfed the firewood. No one told me, but I knew that soon it would be my turn to begin preparing the evening bath.

"I can do that," I said to myself. "Do things fast and easy. Time will fly, and I'll be out of Kapoho before I know it."

One rainy afternoon, I poured kerosene on the wet firewood and watched as the brown bubbles seeped out from the ends. I sat mesmerized, floating away in a gigantic bubble over Kapoho to unknown places. Black smoke stung my eyes and burst my brown bubble. I poured more kerosene, lit a match, threw it on the wet wood and turned away. I had better things to do, returning to the porch and the book I had left facedown on the wooden chair.

After a hard day's work, my father went into the bathhouse, expecting to find a tub of steaming hot water. "The water is cold!" he shouted. "Who made the furo today?" I pretended to be mute and deaf while my brother scurried to restart the fire.

Other times, singed eyebrows and bangs jolted me back to reality. Years later, my younger brother would watch me, and the art of making a furo fire would be passed on.

Coming of age was also just a passage handed down from one child to the next without rites or ceremony. I stood on the concrete floor while my sister soaped me. The tin container that she dipped into the furo disappeared from sight. I prepared my body for the pour of warm water that would fall from above to end this daily ritual. But my mind would never fail to be surprised as the first splashes of the here and now jolted it back from some excursion to the world of wishes.

After getting out of the wooden tub, a brisk toweling and a pat on my butt. A splash on her face for thank-you, and out the door I ran to the next game.

Some of the lessons were all the more significant for the absence of any instruction. What was said in silence wasn't so easy to merely skip away from. Nothing had to be said when my sister began to bathe alone. Her sexuality was screened with silence, and I knew it was time to stay out of her bath. It was the same when I stopped bathing my younger brothers; they didn't need to know why I stopped. I just did.

Throughout my childhood, there were no daughter-and-parent conversations, but superstitions and myths.

"The Kimo-tori will steal your liver if you're outside after dark. In

Japan, children who stay out late are found the next morning without their livers."

"Once in Kapoho," I was further warned, "a child was found near the railroad tracks with her liver missing." The bodies of children with their livers plucked out ran cold in my mind.

It didn't matter if I were in the middle of a favorite game—like kanapio, for instance, the local kids' diversion played like baseball using pieces of wood. The kanapio could be flying through the air, but if the sun were on its last legs, without a word to my friends, I was already halfway home.

The railroad tracks were a dangerous place. "Her body was found by the railroad tracks" was one of the versions of the Kimo-tori stories recounted. In the shadows, beneath the cattle guard of the forbidden crossing, my friend Sammy and I crouched down, listening for the train passing overhead, the hot oil splashing on our heads. A heavy, deep clacking of wheels was a full load of cane being carried to the mill. Other times it would be the tinny rattle of the empty deadhead roaring overhead. But the sound of the sun falling silently below the horizon of cane fields and ōhiā trees screamed louder than the noisiest locomotive. I was out of there, reaching the front porch and checking the road for strange shadows. Without a thought, my body made the journey in an instant and left Sammy to look out for himself. I had my liver to keep.

When it came to telling lies, George and his cherry tree were child's play next to Ema-san. "When you lie, Ema-san will come and cut off your tongue."

"Lemme see, lemme see. I think Ema-san cut off your tongue!" We exposed many liars among neighborhood kids.

"If you leave your clothes hanging out of the bureau drawers, you will have a difficult childbirth" was all my mother said when she saw me put laundry away with pieces of clothing hanging out of the half-closed drawers. I returned to refold my nightgown and properly close the drawers.

Even today, I take a few seconds to put my clothes back into the drawer. I sometimes walk away with a bra strap hanging out of a drawer, but that voice will return me to the bra strap. It's been decades since my childbearing years, but I still glance back after putting the laundry away. One can't be too careful.

Dinner-table manners took only a few sentences.

"You'll turn into a cow if you slouch at the dinner table." No one's taking me out to the pasture.

"That's the emperor's rice! Your eyes will shut if you waste his rice." The starving Chinese families lived in my books. The emperor's rice was on my table.

The road out of Kapoho was long and seemingly endless. I walked out with my liver and eyesight. In my hands, two scholarships and a live-in maid's job for free room and board, and in my pocket, book stories of perfect families, a handbook for future use. I was ready to design and live that storybook all-American life. After all, didn't I raise myself to do all that? Life ought to be easy and fast out of Kapoho.

"I'm out!" I shouted, but it was the first tiny step out of Kapoho.

Taxi Money

She was my mother for 65 years. She was my mother and never told me, "I love you" or that she was proud; she never hugged me or held my hand. Instead, up to the time she was diagnosed with Alzheimer's, she gave me taxi money instead.

I spent all my Christmases with her and put up a tree in her living room, and like a yearly playback recording, I would hear her say with child-like delight, "Ah, Christmas is here, now Santa Claus will come. We can't have Christmas without a tree."

What she really meant was that she needed a tree so that she could enjoy her gifts before Christmas. I first learned of how she was taking a peek at all her gifts when I was in high school. I was sitting under the tree one day, to read the names on the gift tags, when I noticed that the ribbons around her gifts were loosely tied and the wrapping on the bottom of each gift was torn and retaped.

"You opened your presents!" I accused. "You're terrible."

"Shhh," she laughed. "Put them back."

"I'm going to open mine, too," I said. And we became two conspirators, adding a new private tradition to our Christmas.

I never caught her at it when she was carrying out her raids, and she never caught me. We'd accuse each other of being sneaky and bad, and before long, the rest of the family called us "worse than children," two adults unable to wait until Christmas. In later years, they gave us our gifts on Christmas Day, but we had other gifts to rifle.

One Christmas, I added another ritual to our tradition when I conned my mother into giving me the gift of my choice.

"Look at this dress I bought today. Do you want to give this to me for Christmas?"

"You can't buy your own clothes with all the money you make?"

"I'm doing you a favor. This way, you don't need to worry about what to get me for Christmas."

Her comments were always the same as she handed me cash for the cost of my gift.

"You not shame to take money from your poor mother?"

She's been gone since 2002, and I still purchase an extravagant gift from her every Christmas, and I still open my gifts as soon as they arrive.

"What if I die tonight?" I explain to the next generation of nieces and nephews. "I don't want to die not knowing what was in the gift. How sad is that?"

My visits home to my mother's house in Pāhoa ended on the back steps. I would have my carry-on and handbag in hand, ready to leave for the airport. But we would share one more ritual. My mother would hand me a hundred-dollar bill, saying, "Take care. Here's taxi money."

She knew I had a ride from the airport to my apartment, but she'd press the taxi money into my hand. She had been working on a flower farm since my father's death in 1963, seven days a week, holidays included. It was hard work, I knew. She left the house before sunup to catch a ride to the orchid farm. She wore a hat and a white towel over her head and half her face to protect her from the hot sun, and she began her day by picking vanda orchids from plants that were often too high for her to reach. Once the other pickers brought in their first pick, she became the one-person assembly line, weighing and boxing the orchids to keep up with the flower pickers. At the end of each day, she helped to deliver the orchids to Hilo. At home, her labor continued: she raised and sold anthuriums, red ginger flowers, tangerines and navel oranges from her three-acre lot.

"My play money," she'd say. "Otherwise, I starve"—a slight exaggeration.

I earned more money than she did, but no matter how many times she handed me her money, I always took it and said, "Ohhh...taxi money! Thank you." She'd chuckle as I walked down the stairs and waved goodbye, taking her money.

At the airport, I observed a friend hugging her mother. I envied them their intimate moment. I wish I could have done that; I knew my mother would have been delighted, because I'd seen her responses when my nieces and nephews gave her a hug or a kiss, but I was stuck in my upbringing and found it awkward and uncomfortable to break out of that mode.

In later years, there was that taxi money and sometimes a cup of coffee in bed.

For me, mornings were as thick as spilled molasses. In high school I thought of becoming a bank teller, since banks opened after nine, or a waitress who only served lunch and dinner. But after I graduated, I had to put my dreams of sleeping through the mornings on hold, as I became a teacher, living at home the first few years.

On cold winter mornings, I clung deep beneath the covers, beginning with my shouts that echoed through the nearly empty house.

"Somebody! Bring me a cup of coffee! I'm too cold to get up!" Soon footsteps would come from the kitchen.

"Here, you big baby. You not shame to have your poor mother bring you coffee in bed? Better get up. You don't want to speed and get into an accident."

"Would you brush my teeth and wash my face, too?"

Years later, I was living in Honolulu and had a cholycystectomy. My mother flew over and sat all day at my hospital bedside, day after day after day. On the day after surgery, I caught her laughing as she helped me into my new pink robe and matching bedroom slippers.

"What's so funny?" I asked.

She covered her mouth with her hands and tried to stifle her laughter. "I thought only people going on honeymoon bought matching new robe and slippers. This is the hospital, you know."

"You can never tell. Did you get to see the doctor? He looks like a movie star. Don't you want a doctor for a son-in-law?" I held my stitches as I laughed.

Five days later, we went back to my small studio apartment, where we shared the sofa bed and had our meals in my dollhouse of a kitchenette.

"So this is how city people live" was her only comment. We flew back to her home on the Big Island, where I convalesced for the next six weeks. It was a place where birds woke me in the morning and flowers sent their fragrances through the front door, which stayed open during the day and remained unlocked at night. The kitchen was big enough for five couples to waltz and dip. It was a place for deep breathing and healing.

For the next 22 years, I lived in Honolulu and returned home to celebrate our traditional Christmas. Then Alzheimer's crept into our lives and changed everything.

She lived the last years of her life with me in Honolulu, and a new ritual was created: every Saturday, I walked with her at the mall after her hair appointment.

"We're going to the hairdresser" became magical words to speed our mornings. On weekdays, she was prodded and nudged to get dressed for adult day care, but "hairdresser" had her ready within minutes.

For the first time, I held her hand. It was as though we had been holding hands forever. I could feel her ring press into mine. I squeezed her hand, and she chuckled. It was like passing taxi money.

"Look at that." A teenager who was walking through the mall with his friends pointed at us. "Just look at that. That is so awesome. When I'm old, I want my wife or my kid to hold my hand and walk me around the mall like that." His teenage friends were silent. From the looks on their faces, I could almost read, "So what's the big deal about holding hands?"

During the last year of her disease, she didn't recognize me. I hugged her. I massaged her legs and arms. I kissed her forehead. Her speech was gone. My name was gone. Why did I wait so long? Perhaps I waited until her mind was no longer there so that I could finally hug her and show her physical affection without disrespecting and defying that dance we had danced throughout her life. Or was it my dance alone? Silence had always ruled us when it came to expressing our feelings, and I had to believe that she knew that this was the last gesture left for me when language and recognition were no longer available. There were no Christmas gifts to peek into, no walks in the mall, no funny bantering between mother and daughter, not even a chuckle or a cup of hot coffee in bed. All we had between us was a little taxi money. ▣

Ice Fishing

I don't know why Vern invited me to go ice fishing that cold December day in Michigan.

Vern was a farmer, the father of my pen pal Kay, with whom I was living for a year while teaching first graders in Jackson, Michigan. He was a quiet man, like the wintry landscape around me, which revealed very few features. On the few occasions I had dinner at his house, he left the social chatter to his wife and seldom initiated conversations. I knew that I wasn't the most comfortable person for him to welcome into his home, because I had arrived on an alien ship from Hawai'i, with a different face—different enough to raise some concerns among Kay and her neighbors.

A minister stopped me on the street once and offered to sponsor me for U.S. citizenship. A salesclerk spoke slowly, with a long pause between words, "May...I...help...you?" She then kept her eyes on my mouth to lip-read my response. A grocery shop owner ordered a case of Japanese pickles and proudly showed them to me in the back room. I felt obligated to buy a jar each time I entered her shop until the case was empty. I wondered if the rest of the year would be as cautious as the present—polite, welcomed, but as gray and opaque as the weather—until the day Vern gave me one of his prized possessions, and I knew things were about to change.

"I killed this myself," he explained. "I heard you don't have 'em in Hawai'i, so why don't you take this back with you when you return home?" He put the tail of the rattlesnake in my hand. I could still hear its rattle. I screamed and flung the tail away. After the shock and watching that tail fly across the room, I was relieved to know that my host family was as capable of laughing as we in Hawai'i were. We laughed until tears rolled down our faces, and I kept repeating, "I hate snakes. I have a snake phobia." I think we became friends that night.

On the day Vern invited me to go ice fishing, Kay whispered to me, "I hate ice fishing. It's so cold and wet out there. I'd rather be home with a cup of hot cocoa." But I insisted that I was there to explore everything that wasn't found back home, and I wasn't going to miss this chance.

Cautiously I stepped out onto the frozen lake, following Vern like a puppy dog. It was unimaginable that I was walking on a lake. I was already composing a letter home about "walking on water." It was all magic. I was in a child's painting where lines were smeared into indistinct shapes. Nothing stayed inside a line. A dozen shanties, like indistinct old men, appeared to be moving across the lake, or was it the mist? Two fishermen sat around an ice hole in the open, looking like shanties, the only sign of life the fog of their breath becoming clouds close to the ground. The lake was a poem without words.

Vern kept to a straight line. I followed blindly in his tracks.

I wondered how Vern could distinguish his shanty from the others when they all looked so alike. Like a mother penguin hunting for her child, he walked directly toward one. I took a quick look back to where we had come from and saw that the world had closed in behind us, obscure and shrouded in fog. Even if I'd wanted to turn around and go back, there was nowhere to go back to. The lakeshore was lost in mist; everything was silent.

Vern's shanty reminded me of the Kapoho outhouse and my years of sitting there with Sears and Montgomery Ward catalogs, working on my wish list.

"I built this with leftover lumber," he said, sounding like a real estate agent at an open house. "It's not the Hilton, but you'll appreciate it when the winds start to blow." Something warm and familiar crept into my frozen thoughts. The outhouse had been my place of refuge where I'd read adult novels and plotted my escape to become a famous writer.

"Did you build it here?" I asked. "Do you take it down when spring comes?"

He showed me the skids beneath the shanty. "We build them on these skids so we can tow them on and off the lake every year. Last year," he chuckled, "my neighbor waited too long to get his off the lake. He lost his shanty and his truck, too. They both fell into the lake. He was lucky he didn't drown." I was glad it was December.

Once inside the shanty, Vern lighted the portable kerosene heater, which was sitting on a piece of board to keep the ice from melting beneath it. The heat filled the small enclosure with an air of coziness. Vern pointed to one of the stools near the ice hole and motioned me to sit. A perfect host, he poured hot coffee from his thermos and handed it to me as I peered down the hole, which was about 15 inches in diameter. Shadows of fishes swimming deep below darted past.

"Vern, did you ever fall into a hole?" I looked around for a pole to fish me out just in case.

"No, but be careful. Don't get too close. The edge could break off, and you could fall through. It's why we keep the hole small. I've seen whole shanties fall through. But you're safe here."

Vern showed me how to bait the line with live worms that were wriggling in an old tomato can. I hate worms and snakes, but I swallowed hard and baited my own line. "The fish will take a while to find our bait," he explained. "Everything slows down a little under the ice.

"Kay told me you like your fish fried with their heads and tails on. Well, out here, the only way to get 'em like that is to catch 'em yourself."

"Don't worry," I bragged as I carefully fed my line through the hole. "Dinner's going to be on me tonight." We sat on our stools and fished.

To fill the silence, I talked about my father back in Hawai'i, who made his own fishnets. "He has a really good collection of nets," I said. "Lobster nets, toss and cross nets, small- and large-eyed nets for all different-sized fish. I like watching him toss a net over a school of fish. It makes a nice picture, him standing on the black rocks, the ocean all around him. You know, he can spot mullet from a good distance away. He understands the sea and has taught us to respect her. Even today, I don't ever turn my back to the ocean when I'm picking up shells or crabs. Too many people have been washed into the sea when they disregarded the waves. The talk among his buddies is that he knows all the best fishing spots. My father seldom comes home empty-handed. We call it "whitewash" when a person fails to catch any fish."

Vern and I compared ocean fish to the bass and bluegill. "There's nothing like ocean fish, Vern. Lake fish taste bland."

Vern suddenly stood up, and I heard a splash. He yanked his line, and a shiny fish flopped onto the ice. I knocked my stool and mug over, shouting, "You got one! You got one,!"

"Yup," he said. "Pretty good-sized bass, too." He unhooked the fish, put it into the ice chest and baited his line again. We fished in silence for a while longer. Vern cleared his throat.

"Frances," he began, "I heard you're a Buddhist. You know, I never met a Buddhist before, so a few Sundays ago, I told my minister about you. I didn't mean to pry, but I asked my minister what he thought of someone not being a Christian. He said, 'Maybe God sent more than one son down to us.' I've been thinking about that. It makes a lot of sense to me. What do you think?"

"I never thought about it," I said. "All I know is that we attend church to become better people, so it really shouldn't matter what church we attend."

"Well," Vern said, "I felt good about what the minister said. I thought Jesus was the only way to salvation. The minister's words eased my mind a lot, with you being Buddhist and all that."

"That's good, Vern. You wouldn't want to be out here fishing with a pagan savage."

Our laughter filled the shanty, and soon the conversation passed to other matters and left us quietly engaged in a question-and-question dialogue. I asked him about fishing and farming and local gossip, and he wanted to know more about Hawai'i, the one he knew through Jack Lord and *Hawaii Five-0*.

I sat drifting, watching bluegill and bass swim beneath the frozen lake. It felt right, my farmer friend and me, here on the frozen lake in that cozy little shack. It was like living inside a Frost poem, a place that didn't need my voice or my words. This would be the first Christmas I'd be spending away from home.

Christmas at my mother's always brought her adult children back home. Their families came with their mixed ethnic potluck: Filipino pansit, Korean kalbi, Japanese sushi and sashimi, and other international dishes prepared from new recipes. A house full of laughter, and a lot of teasing among young cousins who hadn't seen each other since the last holiday. These spontaneous sounds seemed to be reserved for the young as the adults watched with amusement from the sidelines, except for my mother.

A burst of laughter and shouts from the living room caught my attention.

"Grandma! I didn't know you knew such words!"

"Wow, Grandma, some mouth!"

"Grandma, you're all right!"

"What?" I heard my mother's voice say again. "You think Grandma don't know what a 'cocksucka' is? Eh, don't take me so cheap. Of course I know what a 'cocksucka' is."

Two nieces ran into the kitchen to where I stood over the sink.

"Aunty Fran! Aunty Fran! Do you know what Grandma said? You won't believe this! This is just awesome! She said 'cocksucker.' She told us not to be 'cocksuckers.'"

"Hey," I said, aware of the generation gap being displayed. "Grandma is really sharp, you know. Don't underestimate her." "Cocksucka" means "tattler" in Kapoho pidgin, and I decided that some things were better left unexplained. Instead I added, "She watches a lot of soap opera so is pretty up-to-date."

After the leftover food and dishes were put away, my nieces, my nephew and I walked around the neighborhood, talking story, playing catch-up. Back on the porch, we sat, talked more story and watched the younger children play.

The day ended with my mother and me standing at the bottom of the steps, waving at each car as its headlights swept across the driveway. We stayed until the last car was completely out of sight. I still hear my mother's voice saying, "*Yo-katta, yo-katta,*" it was good, it was good, as we walked back up the steps.

The house was silent now. Just the two of us, and I felt empty and disconnected. It was a familiar feeling that would accompany me on my flight home. It would be days before it blended into the mist of previous gatherings.

My siblings and I were close, growing up in that old house. I missed the closeness of those times and felt the sadness of leaving them. As the years went by, even Christmas began to feel like a goodbye. Conversations turned into scripts, just scraps repeated over and over at each gathering, fillers for the silence in between.

"How are you? Fine. How's work? Good. What's new? Oh, nothing much."

I wished I could have rewritten the script a bit differently: "What is life really like for you? Are you happy? Who have you become? Do you know who I am?"

But in all likelihood, we probably would have answered, "Fine, fine. Good, good. Oh, nothing much."

Splash! There was water all over my face! I screamed and covered my face with both hands. Vern pulled another fish out of the lake, and I watched the end of my fishing line disappear through the hole.

"Oh, no, Vern. I lost my line."

"Here, use my line. I'll get another one." I attached a new worm to the hook and dropped it back through the hole.

"Vern, I don't feel a nibble. I think they're teasing me. 'Catch me if you can.'"

"Gotta be patient, Frances."

I sat entranced, seeing only glimpses of fish: their tails and heads darting beneath the hole, which was too small to display their whole bodies.

"Hey, Vern, look at all those fish," I said, holding the line with one hand and pointing down with the other. "It's magic that we're sitting here on ice and all that life is going on underneath. Do you think our lives are like this? We live on the surface and never really know what goes on with people? Maybe we need to crack ice now and then."

Vern didn't reply and continued to fish. I wondered if he had heard me. After awhile, he finally said, "Well, if you want to do that, you'd better know how to swim."

I felt by the look on his face that whether Buddha was a son or not was the only serious discussion we would have that day. Other than that, we were ice fishing; that was all. Yet there was something about being there in that silence, watching life beneath the surface. It made me feel that the fish were not the only ones being lured to the surface. I felt the same nostalgia that often came to me on late Sunday afternoons, a feeling that has no name.

My mother was sitting in the garage on a stool, cleaning tangerines and navel oranges, while I roamed the house trying to recapture the poet who'd been playing hide-and-seek. I'd dreamed of this day my entire life. I'd had a book signing in Hilo for my first published book of poems, *Sand Grains*. That was a big time for a country bumpkin: a story in two newspapers, a bouquet of flowers from the mayor, curious strangers in line for autographed copies and a continuous flow of family and friends bearing leis and gifts.

We'd celebrated that day, and I was a celebrity. I'd wanted to stay there forever, but even celebrities eventually go home. The drive back to Pāhoa was not long enough to transform a poet back into the ordinary me who had chores waiting. I was still rehearsing an acceptance speech in Stockholm for the Nobel Prize as I drove into the driveway.

Sunday afternoons were orange-picking days for us. My mother and I washed and boxed the fruit for the market. This particular Sunday was no different, except for the fact that I was still somewhere onstage, taking another bow.

My mother greeted me with, "I can do this myself. Go into the house. You don't have to do this today." That was all the excuse I needed. I was moved that my mother understood and knew that the poet was still hanging around.

"Frances," I heard Vern laugh. "Maybe you need to put a pineapple around your hook. Your fish aren't biting." He pulled another fish out up through the hole.

"I'm waiting for the big one, Vern. I need a bigger hole."

"Maybe you should dance the hula, Frances."

Early in my teaching career, I worked as a supervisor of teachers. I was young and inexperienced, and on numerous afternoons I went home complaining, "Those idiot teachers! They don't understand! What's wrong with them?" My mother listened and said nothing.

Not long afterward, my mother returned from Hilo with a beautiful porcelain Noh mask of a woman, delicately wrapped in white tissue paper. She took it out of the box, pointed to different parts of the mask and recited in poetic Japanese verse, "There is almost no chin. This is so that one can see one's feet and keep one's head down. The cheeks are high, so one can't look at the neighbors with envy. The forehead sticks out, so one can't turn one's nose up in the air." She handed the mask to me and said, "This is for you, Hideko." I took the mask and hung it on my bedroom wall. On quiet mornings, it looked at me or I looked at it. That mask would follow me for many years.

The chill in the air prompted us to stop fishing. The heater was out of kerosene, and the sun would be setting in a couple of hours. We pulled our lines out of the lake, had one last mug of coffee and got our gear together.

"I'm sorry you were whitewashed, Frances," Vern apologized.

I took one last look into the ice hole.

"I didn't need to catch any fish today, Vern."

A One-Chopstick Marriage

The sun was relentless. Sadame looked at the two piles from his morning's work. The more he cut, the bigger his paycheck. He took another two swipes, removing the stalk on the forward slash and the leafy top on the backward stroke, and tossed the cane stalk onto his second pile. He made his signature knot from a cane leaf to identify his stack and tucked it on the top of the pile.

Rhythmic chopping punctuated the grating noise of cane loaders in the adjoining field, lifting tons of cane onto trucks for transport to the mill. Shouts from truck drivers and cane operators giving directions filled the air. By noon, half the cane field looked like a wheat farm after harvest, with mounds of sugar-cane distributed like bales of hay.

Sweat rolled down Sadame's face. His denim shirt, a second skin, was wet against his back. His shoulders and arms were stiff and aching. He didn't think he could get another swing out of his cane knife before lunch. He looked up at the sun and waited for the lunch whistle. When it sounded, a tent of silence covered the field. The trucks and cane loaders turned off their engines, cane cutters put their cane knives down and shouts dropped to muffled voices.

Sadame reached for his denim lunch bag from the branch of a guava tree and sat down with Masa and Pedro and the other cane cutters. Masa, his occasional drinking partner after work, had been Sadame's closest friend since boyhood. Pedro, a Filipino immigrant, had recently sent for a wife from the Philippines, after working for the plantation for more than seven years. Nicknamed "Ten-ga-la," "Empty Tin Can," by Masa because of his continuous chatter, he was tiresome at times, especially when overworked bodies wanted silence.

Sadame lifted the two-layered stainless steel lunch pail out of his bag. In the bottom layer was the usual white rice with an ume pressed into the top. The juice bled a dark rose circle into the rice; he imagined his wife before bed, letting her kimono drop from her shoulders and pool at her feet.

"Eh, Sadame-san, I like change lunch with you. My wife only put rice and shoyu in my lunch. Your wife put good stuff every day."

Pedro was right about his lunch. The beads of water lining the pail told Sadame that his rice was freshly cooked, just as it was every morning. Matsue got up long before him; he never heard a sound. His hot tea and breakfast would be waiting for him on the kitchen table while she woke the children up for school. Before he could finish the last of his tea, she'd be standing by the door with his lunch bag in hand.

Sadame had worried when he first brought Matsue to Kapoho as his new bride. How would she take to a place that had no electricity or water system? Would she be able to use the outhouse? If she had complaints, she didn't tell him.

Every morning had found her sitting on a stool in the front of the woodstove, waiting for the rice to cook, fanning the air to keep the flames hot. An hour later, the coals would be embers, and his hot breakfast of rice and tea would be waiting for him on the table. When he returned in the afternoon, a hot, steamy furo would be ready. The glass chimneys of the kerosene lamps sparkled every night when she lighted the wicks at sundown. The woodstove was later replaced by a kerosene stove and then a gas stove, but it didn't change her routine. It was as if there were several versions of her around the house all at once.

Kapoho was isolated from other towns, and travel meant an hour's train ride to Hilo. It was an all-day event. Staples like Spam, Vienna sausage, flour, canned sardines, rice and sugar were ordered through the Hara store in another village. Other items like cigarettes, beer and bread could be found at any of the four small grocery stores in Kapoho.

"Never forget Mr. Hara," Matsue told her children. "Mr. Hara never charges interest on our account."

Occasionally, a meat vendor from Hilo rumbled into the village to sell pork and beef from the back of his refrigerated truck. A piece of steak or pork cooked with vegetables would feed a family of seven along with the visitors who often dropped by around dinnertime.

If he could have read her mind, he would have heard a private wish: "I wonder if the day will ever come when I'll be able to have a whole steak or piece of pork to myself." She kept her wishes to herself until many years later, when she spoke them to her grown children each time full portions of steaks or pork chops were put in front of her at mealtime.

"Oh, shit!" complained Masa. "I got fried eggs again. What did your wife cook, Sadame?"

He opened the top layer of his pail and found fried fish that he had caught the evening before. Three fanned slices of lemon rested on top of the fish, with a mound of pickled cucumbers and daikon in a pool of shoyu sauce at its side. Slices of sweet navel oranges were carefully wrapped in waxed paper. They filled his nostrils with their refreshing scent.

He reached for his chopsticks from the separate pocket that his wife had sewn on his lunch bag. The first time Pedro and Masa had seen the lunch bag, they had teased him about having a fancy dressmaker for a wife.

Sadame was proud that his wife was a dressmaker and not a field worker like many of the women in the village. He had built two shelves against the living room wall where she kept all the customers' material and Sears and Montgomery Ward catalogs. Under the shelves was a large wooden table on which she spread wrapping paper to draft clothes patterns. Protruding from the wall and to one side was a nail to hang a yardstick and a square, and in an adjoining room was a manual sewing machine. Sadame knew his wife was good at what she did, and he provided her with whatever she needed.

People brought in pictures of dresses from which she created exact replicas. It was not uncommon to see two or three children at school all wearing original dresses made from the same material. The material would come from a vendor who brought bolts of cloth, buttons, threads and zippers to the village. Her work compared fairly with the best store-bought clothes, although she and her sister-in-law often paraded in hand-painted clothes shipped from Japan or Honolulu.

She taught drafting and sewing to young single ladies in the village. Men, women, children and plantation managers all came to her living room to talk story as well as do business. Train engineers dropped by with pants to be shortened or mended. She had a reputation for sewing the most comfortable pair of men's pants in the village.

"Ah, Mama," a Filipino confessed to her once. "My wife come from Philippine Island. When she iron your pants, she speak, 'Who make this pants? This pants easy to iron.' She like your pants, Mama. She ask if you can sew her clothes, too."

"Right, now, you stand straight," she told him, applying the square to the inner seam of his pants. She pressed the square against his inner thigh.

"Silly man," she scolded. "You think I want to measure your penis? You don't have enough to measure! Stand still. If I measure wrong, your wife won't be happy with my work. She won't send you back."

While Sadame was at work, her door was always open to the comings and goings of friends and clients. She quickly became the village confidante.

Young men and women often asked for love advice while others, many of them immigrants from the Philippines, viewed her as a trusted friend.

"They lie like hell, Mama!" one Filipino laborer complained, showing her a page from the Sears catalog. "I order this girl from this book, but they no send the girl, they send me only the clothes."

"Bakatare!" she told him.

Soon, "Ask Mrs. Kakugawa" became a common refrain in the village.

Two ladies from the Buddhist church sat in her living room. After formal exchanges of bows and salutations, one of them said, "Kakugawa-san, we need someone to greet the people at our conference. We need someone to speak in both English and Japanese for the first generation and the younger generation. Will you do this for us?"

It was not long before Matsue was elected president of the Buddhist Women's Group and attended monthly meetings and conferences in other towns.

Once a group of girls approached her to start a Girl Scout troop in Kapoho. She couldn't refuse their plea, "You're the only person who can do this. Please do this for us." Like all the troops, Matsue's Girl Scouts got their uniforms from the usual official sources. But after Matsue's fittings and alterations, they were the best-dressed troop in the district. They would proudly venture out of Kapoho to meet other troops in Hilo.

It made Sadame uneasy that she was spending more time outside of the house. It wasn't what he had had in mind. He was proud when villagers thanked him for having his wife be the leader of their daughters' Girl Scout troop, but along with praise came criticism, sometimes heard in the fields.

"Eh, Sadame-san. You some lucky, your wife cook different food for you every day. I have Spam and rice three times this week. Maybe your wife can show my wife how to cook."

It would be so easy if life were a good lunch. It was what he had meant it to be when he and Mr. Sato had gone to ask for her hand in marriage. Why would he want her to be like other wives?

Mr. Sato, Sadame's marriage go-between, had sat across from Mr. Takahashi on the tatami mat. Sadame had sat next to him, his right hand clasping his left and resting uneasily on his lap. He could hear his own breathing and his heart beating a little faster than usual. He was hoping that Mr. Takahashi would accept his request to marry Mr. Takahashi's sister. He was almost 29 now, and it was time he married and settled down. Mr. Sato had assured him that Matsue would make an ideal wife for him.

"She's only eighteen, but she's a good catch, Sadame. Her parents came from Hiroshima, like you. She's from a good family, there's no mental illness, no leprosy, no criminals. Her sister married into a respectable family. She's attending Mrs. Nako's sewing school, and she works on the plantation. A hard worker, Sadame. She finished more school than you, all the way to fifth grade. She's very well brought up, too. You will like her, Sadame.

"Now we just have to see if her brother will like you. There have already been two other suitors. Takahashi rejected them, but I think he will accept you. You are an honest man, Sadame. And you have a good sense of humor, too! Yes, Sadame, I think he will approve."

The house was a well-kept two-story plantation home, with a large garden and room for some chickens and small farm animals. The furnishings were spare: tatami mats, low tables and cushions. A teakettle was steaming in one corner of the room. Mr. Takahashi's mother poured them some tea and left the room. The men could hear muffed voices at the bottom of the stairs.

After some small talk and a few sips of tea, Mr. Sato came to the point. "Takahashi-san, Sadame has a good job with the sugar plantation. He owns his own house, he is an oldest son, and his parents came from Hiroshima, like your parents."

Mr. Takahashi received his guests' petition in silence. When Mr. Sato had finished, Mr. Takahashi thought for a few moments. Then he called out to the open door, "Matsue! Will you come upstairs a moment?" Matsue had been lingering at the bottom of the stairs ever since the men began their conversation. Her soft footsteps could be heard on the creaking stairway as she made her way up to the landing. "Come in, Matsue, and meet our guests."

Sadame cleared his throat in nervousness as Matsue pushed aside the shoji. She stood at the entrance for a moment. Sadame coughed and smiled.

Matsue was dressed in drab work clothes that covered her from head to toe. A white scarf completely covered her head and half of her face. She stepped into the room. Only a glimpse of her cheeks and the long, slender fingers pressed to her side gave hints of the exquisitely creamy complexion that was hidden beneath her loose-fitting garments.

"This one has spunk," Sadame thought, glancing at her.

"Matsue, we have guests! What is this?" Mr. Takahashi scolded. Matsue proceeded to bow respectfully to the guests as Mr. Takahashi introduced them to the prospective bride. Mr. Sato laughed and steadied his teacup.

Sadame looked at her again. A silly notion flitted through his mind. "Do ghosts," he thought, "not change their work clothes when they come in from the fields?" The thought passed, and Sadame politely returned Matsue's bow.

"Matsue," Mr. Takahashi continued, "this is Mr. Kakugawa and his go-between, Mr. Sato." Matsue and the visitors exchanged bows again. Matsue then took her place on a cushion at one side of the entry.

"They have come with a proposal for marriage. I am considering the matter."

Mr. Takahashi looked closely at her. He saw her hands open slightly and her shoulders relax a little. She gave a slight bow.

Mr. Takahashi excused his sister, and she silently rose to her feet, bowed to the guests and left the room. He turned to Mr. Sato and Sadame and said, "If we are still in agreement, I have decided to accept your proposal of marriage to my sister."

Sadame's hands relaxed, and his shoulders dropped slightly. A brief exhalation indicated his relief that the matter had been favorably decided. Mr. Sato reached out and placed his hand on Sadame's knee, as if to say, "Not quite, Sadame." Then he leaned forward and spoke to Mr. Takahashi in a confidential tone. "Well, Takahashi-san, all seems to be settled then, except there is one small thing."

"What might that be, Sato-san?"

"Your sister appears to be a wonderful match for Sadame, and I think they would do very well together. Would you agree?"

"Yes, Sato-san, I certainly do, or else I wouldn't have given my consent."

"But Takahashi-san, don't you think it is very hard to buy fish already wrapped in thick brown paper?"

"Ah, but Sato-san, if you know that the fishmonger sells nothing but freshly caught fish, does it matter that you can't see the fish? Besides," Mr. Takahashi added, "I happen to know, Sato-san, that you were at our Obon dance last year and paid some particular attention to Matsue's obvious charms. So I don't really think it is any surprise to you that she is an exceptionally graceful and companionable woman."

The men laughed, and the air of formality melted away. They finished their tea and said their mutual goodbyes, and Mr. Sato and Sadame descended the stairs. At the bottom, the two men looked briefly for a glimpse of Matsue to offer their respects before leaving. But she was nowhere in sight. Mr. Sato squeezed Sadame's shoulder and said, "Never mind, you will have a lifetime to regard your new bride."

"Eh, Sadame-san!" Pedro interrupted. "Your wife is a good dancer, I hear. My Emma say your wife dance at the PTA meeting last night. She even dance with the plantation manager. Said she dance the bosses under the table. I wish my wife like that. My wife snore right after dinner."

"Ten-ga-la, Ten-ga-la," Masa said, shaking his head. "I would sleep, too, if I were your wife."

Sadame stopped listening to their rattle and reached into his lunch bag where his black lacquered chopsticks would be.

He should have known that the woman he married was not typical of Japanese women of the time.

"People are talking about you," he'd told her. "Why did you use that umbrella when it wasn't raining? I heard Mr. Doi say, 'Look at her, using an umbrella and it's not even raining. She must think she's the empress or something.'" She hadn't defended her act, but she hadn't put her sun umbrella away.

He should have known that she would not live a quiet, unassuming, obedient life within the confines of their marriage.

"Don't be president of the Women's Group again," he'd told her a month ago. "One time 'nuff. Let other ladies be president. I heard other women want to be president." She hadn't said a word then. Last night she'd announced that she'd been elected for another term.

"I told you not to be president again!" He'd looked at her in anger and walked out of the room. She'd watched him leave without saying a word.

He should have known that she was not going to listen to any voice of authority. He should have known that. Her brother had told him about the Strike Boss when they were drinking, months after the wedding.

She, 17 years old at the time, had been working in the cane fields with a group of girls. She couldn't be recognized, because all the girls covered their heads with white towels to keep their faces from tanning. A porcelain white face had been considered an attribute of beauty as far back as medieval Japan, when women painted their faces white.

A luna accused them of being lazy. Never did a word of praise escape his mouth. "You lazy, good-for-nothing wahine! Work faster! You work too slow!" After months of being abused like this, Matsue gathered all the workers around her.

"That man is pushing us too much without giving us a break. Let's have a sit-down strike. Tomorrow, after lunch, we just sit. We don't work."

"Matsue-san, you sure we won't get fired?"

"Don't worry. Just follow me. They can't fire us."

The next day, the women did exactly that. She told the luna they needed more break time. "Baka! Stupid!" he sputtered. "Go back to work!"

After lunch, they didn't go back to work.

"Get back to work! Why are you sitting like lazy jackasses?" the luna shouted.

The women sat for an hour. They said nothing. Their act of defiance brought no changes, but Matsue earned the secret title "the Strike Boss."

Their job under the hot sun was to gather all the loose cane stalks left behind after the cane loaders had taken the piles of cane to the mill. The women would gather these stalks and toss them into the flumes. The flumes, filled with gushing water, would transport the cane to the mill. The luna's verbal abuse continued and pushed them beyond their limits.

"Enough. Let's clog the flumes," the Strike Boss said one day. She organized the women into small groups, and they piled stalks of cane crosswise and ran up and down the flumes, building beaver dams to stop the flow of suagrcane. Eventually, all work was stopped as supervisors ran along the flumes to determine the cause of the clogs. The women sat down and looked on.

"Goddam! Who stuck up the flumes?" The luna was met with silence. A few voices whispered, "The Strike Boss." The flumes continued to clog under the leadership of the mysterious Strike Boss, and the women got their breaks.

"The Strike Boss was no fool," thought Sadame.

He took one chopstick out of the bag. Then he reached into his bag and felt around for its match. He turned the bag inside out. There was still only one chopstick. He looked around him. Perhaps it had fallen out.

"Aiya! Only one chopstick."

"Eh, Sadame-san. Your wife think you Filipino. You gotta eat with your fingers," teased Pedro.

Before her marriage, Matsue had been sent to a strict sewing school where she learned to draft and sew clothes. Between the drafting and sewing lessons, she had heard lectures on how to be a good and obedient wife.

"Well-brought-up girls get up early in the morning and never sleep in, even on weekends and holidays. Only the sick stay in bed during the day. The first bowl of rice from the center of the pot goes to the man of the house. A hot furo must always be ready when the husband returns from work. Don't answer back. We are here to serve husbands." And she did.

She was no complainer. She'd stand by quietly while he and his friends emptied a gallon of saké and continued long into the night. She always made sure he had a pack of Camels and a bottle of sake. During the rationing days, she would stand in line to get liquor and cigarettes.

There was only one chopstick. Sadame laid the chopstick on the ground beside him. He looked at it for a moment. Then he rose, took his knife, went to a nearby guava tree and cut a slim branch. He measured it against the chopstick and made it the same length.

It was during their second meeting at a train station in Hilo, after her brother had accepted his marriage proposal to her, that he had first seen her face. She didn't say much with Mr. Sato and her brother as chaperones, but she didn't have that towel over her face.

He never told her she was beautiful, but he often told his sons, "When you choose a wife, be sure it's someone you're proud to be seen with while walking the sidewalks of Hilo."

His children told her what he couldn't say: "Ohhhh, he must be so proud of you, you must be so beautiful." He knew she enjoyed these moments by the sparkle in her eyes, although she only rebutted, "Say whatever you like."

"Eh, Sadame-san, you need help? You drop your food. I think better eat with fingers. Your chopstick no match." Pedro's voice led him to look at his lunch. A piece of fish was on his lap. He looked at his chopsticks. They were not a good match with one part of the guava stick bent outward, but he was able to bring food to his mouth, at least most of it.

He had seen her for the third time on their wedding day. She was dressed in her traditional Japanese wedding kimono complete with a headdress, white tabi and brocaded lacquer clogs. She rode with her mother, her sister and brother, and their families on a train from Onomea to remote Kapoho. When she arrived at the house, the hemline of her kimono was soaked in brown mud. It had been all thunder and storms since dawn.

The neighbors were there out of curiosity to see the newest bride of Kapoho. He felt a few feet taller when he heard the women murmuring, "She is so beautiful." The men slapped him on his back and exclaimed, "You sure caught a beauty."

At the end of the wedding day, after the guests had left and the party dishes had all been put away, he found himself alone with his new wife. She sat quietly on the floor near the bridal futon with her head down. "Come to bed," he gently coaxed her.

He didn't know how else to handle the situation. Where was that feisty woman who had covered her face with the cloth? Was she still hiding?

"Come to bed." She slowly approached the futon. She untied the sash around her waist and slipped out of her kimono. He moved to one side of the futon, and without a word, she crawled under the cover.

During the next ten years, they had five children, three sons and two daughters. Each time it thundered and stormed, he told the story of Matsue sitting away from the bridal bed and how he'd had to coax her. It was his favorite story to tell on rainy days. Her stories focused on the mud on her bridal kimono.

"I think Sadame-san made his wife mad last night. When my wife mad at me, she put only rice and shoyu in my lunch."

"I think she put one chopstick on purpose."

More laughter. A frown appeared on Sadame's face for only a second. He put his empty lunch pail into the bag. Then he took his homemade chopstick and aligned it against the lacquer stick as best he could, with the guava stick bent at one end. He took a thin strip of cane leaf and tied the sticks together with his signature knot. He placed them carefully into the pocket of his lunch bag and closed it.

There would be many more one-chopstick lunches.

I was raised in my parents' one-chopstick marriage, where loud silence and subtlety ruled. Among my flatware of forks and knives today, there is always that one chopstick. After all, I am my parents' daughter. ▩

Mrs. Honda's Beautiful Daughter

When Mrs. Honda died, one of my two faces was buried with her.

It's a mystery how messages were received in small plantation villages where there were no private telephones, local newsletters or community bulletin boards. In Kapoho, a village of fewer than a thousand people, the following message from the plantation hospital was delivered to every household where a five-year-old lived:

"All children entering first grade should have their tonsils removed by Dr. McKenzie."

Even at five years old, I was suspicious of the hospital and Dr. McKenzie. They called him "Horse Doctor." No matter what the symptoms, when villagers went to his office, they walked out with the same pills. Soon they would share them with other family members. It saved more trips to the hospital.

"Horse Doctor" or not, he was the only doctor available, unless my parents borrowed someone's car to drive us to a private doctor in Hilo. Even so, city doctors were viewed with some suspicion. And besides, Horse Doctor was cheaper.

When my ten-year-old sister complained of a severe stomach ache, my parents decided that this was too serious for the plantation doctor and took her to Hilo. Within minutes the physician made his diagnosis: "It's her appendix; it needs to come out today."

My mother thanked him, hurried my sister out of the office and took her to Mrs. Yamada, the village midwife and witch doctor. Mrs. Yamada had been there when my mother's water broke and my brother was coming out feet first. Mrs. Yamada had magic in her hands; a little massage, and my brother turned and came out right side up. That was why my mother took my sister to Mrs. Yamada that day.

"No, no," Mrs. Yamada said, after pressing my sister's stomach. "No need for surgery. Yaito will fix this." She marked a spot on my sister's arm and instructed, "Burn six yaito three times a day on this spot until pain is gone."

Yaito was a simple remedy, though extremely painful. Mugwort herbs called moxa, aged and ground into a fluff like lint from a dryer, were a staple in most Japanese medicine cabinets. My mother placed a pearl-sized fluff of moxa on the spot marked on my sister's arm and lit it. A tiny flame engulfed the moxa and burned itself out. She repeated this six times. My sister did not even whimper. After all, being burned was better than having someone cut your stomach open. She had no problem with her appendix after the yaito treatment, though she still bears a burn scar to this day.

For cuts and bruises and other ailments, we would go to our neighbor Nalani for her native Hawaiian medicine. For diarrhea, we chewed the young leaves of the guava plant and swallowed the bitter juice. For cuts and scrapes, we chewed the young shoots, then applied them to the open wounds to stop the bleeding. Squatting over the steam of burning fig leaves cured hemorrhoids, and a piece of aloe worked as well as a suppository.

One day, my father fell off the roof and lost consciousness for a few minutes. Nalani gave him a cup of warm water mixed with Hawaiian sea salt. He recovered completely.

But when the message about tonsillectomies buzzed around the village, we all paid attention. "Horse Doctor" or not, Dr. McKenzie was still the voice of medical authority, so I was on his waiting list, too, along with other five-year-olds in Kapoho.

Mrs. Honda, one of the mothers in the village, placed even greater faith in doctors, or anyone with a title before his or her name. She scheduled her daughter Hiroko to be the first to have her tonsils out that summer.

News of Hiroko's surgery traveled rapidly. There would be no other tonsillectomy that year. Hiroko died on the operating table. Horse Doctor had overdosed her with ether. Needless to say, I still have my tonsils today.

The villagers, dressed in black suits and dresses, showed up for Hiroko's funeral service at the Honda home. Hiroko's casket was surrounded by orchids and azaleas from people's yards. The scent of incense and the soft Buddhist sutra from the priest greeted me when I entered the room with my mother. Imitating my mother, I went up to the Buddhist shrine next to the casket, lit a stick of incense and placed it upright in the incense urn with all the others. I put my hands together in prayer, with my own rosary called o-juzu around both my hands, and followed my mother to Mrs. Honda.

Mrs. Honda was weeping, "What shall I do? What shall I do?" to everyone who offered condolences. No one had an answer. Hiroko had been her youngest child. Hiroko was irreplaceable. Mrs. Honda was inconsolable.

When it was my turn, Mrs. Honda reached out and touched my face. "Hiroko, Hiroko, *honto ni kawai,*" truly precious, so beautiful. Before

I could say anything, someone pulled on my skirt and hurried me along. But it was too late. In that brief moment, I became two daughters.

A few months later, I passed Mrs. Honda on the way to the store. She stared at me and then began to weep and said, "If Hiroko were alive, she would look like you." I stared back at her without saying a word.

During my teens, whenever we met, Mrs. Honda would look at my face and say, "What a beautiful face. Hiroko would look exactly like you." In those years, I looked like a photo on a CARE package, in loosely fitted homemade dresses and a haircut styled by my father's scissors. Mrs. Honda never noticed. She'd say, "Just look at your flawless complexion." She was mercifully blind to my freckles and pimples, my small "single-eyes" and skinny body. My family teased me each time I ran home bragging, "I saw Mrs. Honda, and she said I was beautiful."

"Yeah," my brother Paul laughed, "just like a morning glory, all dried up at the end of the day." To this day, Paul still calls me "MG."

Mrs. Honda worked as a laborer in the cane fields. Whenever I saw her in her work clothes, with a towel covering half her face to protect it from the sun, she was full of apologies and embarrassed to have me see her in her oversized, long-sleeved denim shirt, her pants tied at the waist with a cord. On her feet were denim Japanese tabi with rubber soles.

"Look at me in these work clothes," she'd say. "Look at my face, so dark and ugly. But look at you. Your face is so beautiful. Hiroko would look like you today."

I accepted her compliments with a smile. Mrs. Honda had just outshouted the boys in the hallway, the same boys who hid *Playboy* under their mattresses, the ones who whispered, "Eh, Stew Bones" as I passed by, clutching my oversized jacket to my chest.

To have discounted this compliment, even from a naive and simple woman, would have denied Mrs. Honda her image of Hiroko and would have denied Stew Bones the confidence to take off her jacket. I wonder if Mrs. Honda knew what a lift she gave me that day.

Mrs. Honda also extended her family by one other member: my father. He occasionally worked with Mr. Honda on the papaya farm after his retirement from the sugar plantation. One day, he returned home from work saying, "That silly woman. Today she packed a lunch for me, too."

"Ohhh," I teased, "she has a crush on you."

We all knew that Mrs. Honda checked the work schedule, and on days when Mr. Honda and my father worked together, she would pack fancy lunches with food usually reserved for New Year's Day: sushi, shrimp tempura and nishime.

"Look at that bakatare woman," Mr. Honda would say. "I don't know what got into her." And then he'd spread her lunch for the two of them. Mr. Honda allowed Mrs. Honda these simple pleasures, chalking them up to his wife's continuing grief.

Whenever I saw Mrs. Honda going past our house with her head down, I'd call out to my father, "Come quick. Come quick. Your girlfriend is passing." I could tell that Mrs. Honda didn't want to be noticed in her dirty work clothes.

My father would chuckle, "You can say whatever you like."

When my father died, Mrs. Honda was the first to arrive from the neighborhood to offer her condolences. She openly wept and called out my father's name. I was older then and held her to me. We hugged each other as if we'd always been doing that.

A few weeks before my high school graduation, my photo appeared in the *Hilo Tribune Herald* because of a scholarship that I had received. The next day, Mrs. Honda stopped me on the roadside and said, "If Hiroko were alive, she'd be just like you. Smart and beautiful."

In Mrs. Honda's eyes, Hiroko accompanied me to college, and we both became teachers. After graduating from college, I didn't see much of Mrs. Honda in Kapoho, but when I did, she would always say, "Hiroko would have become a teacher just like you."

On one occasion, she said, "How lucky you have a tall nose, just like a haole. Look at your white complexion, just like a haole. You are truly beautiful." I was a college graduate, a grown woman, but still I had the urge to return home to tell the family, "Mrs. Honda still thinks I'm beautiful."

When my first four books were published, Mrs. Honda attended each of my book signings. Though she was issei like my grandmothers and had never learned to read or write in Japanese or English, she bought my books, held them in both hands and bowed.

Why she chose me among all the girls in the village I will never know. But to Mrs. Honda, the child who became her surrogate daughter was the most beautiful child in Kapoho. Her face glowed with love and affection when she looked at me, and I accepted her praises with a smile.

When Hiroko had died, there were whispers in the village that it could have been a blessing. "She would have struggled in school," people said. They did not believe that Hiroko could ever have become an independent adult or have met someone someday who would have accepted her as his wife. Children had teased Hiroko. They called her "Mochi-Face," as they once called me "Stew Bones."

Someday when my face turns into a wadi bed, my skin is mottled with dark liver spots and my hair is sparse and gray, I want to hear Mrs. Honda saying once more, "Hideko-san, you are beautiful." ▣

Akira's Flashlight: A Kapoho Story

He was dying, but it was different this time. His frail body lay between two clean sheets, and a lamp lit the room, casting soft shadows on the white walls. Murmured voices played like a gentle sonata in the background. His right hand, mapped with blue veins from years of labor, was held in two warm hands. Around him, a familiar fragrance brought comfort, as it had for the past 40 years.

He had been five years old the first time. The room had been dark except for the dim light from a kerosene lamp. His little body was curled on a mattress covered with sheets that were thin and frayed from too many scrubbings on the washing board. He had been in bed for over a week, listening to faint voices outside his door. His mother's tired face and his father's stern look hovered over him during his moments of consciousness. He didn't know what was happening, only that he was tired, and his coughing kept him up throughout the night.

The doctor's weather-beaten hand pressing into his body told him nothing except that he was in pain. He didn't understand the sob torn out of his mother when the doctor quietly shook his head. His father left the room, taking the lamp with him.

He rested in the dark, knowing there was fear lurking in the room. That was all he knew. Then he heard his father's voice. His father had entered the room again and had sat on a chair that squeaked like hinges needing oil.

"Akira-chan, I will get you a present. What do you want?" For a moment Akira thought he had misheard his father. His father's voice was filled with tenderness. His father had never called him "Akira-chan." It was always a harsh "Akira!" Presents? He had never received one except for an orange one Christmas morning.

His eyes met his father's, and he stuttered, "A-a-a flashlight." His father stood up and left the room. When Akira awoke during the night, the moonlight through the curtainless window shone on an object near his bed. He reached out and grasped a flashlight. A flashlight.

He flicked it on and delighted at the beam of light. He pointed it to the ceiling from his bed. He moved the beam from one side of the room to the other. Like magic, he seemed to hold the entire room together in that one sweeping moment. Even the ceiling didn't seem so far away. He turned the switch to "off" and then to "on" again, feeling he had total control over the darkness. The shadows that had teased and threatened him no longer existed. He pulled the old blanket over his head and held the flashlight high in his little tent, and night was gone. Dragons and monsters disappeared, and his heart soared like the tail of a kite in the blue sky.

"Akira!" jolted him out of his tent. His father was standing next to his bed. "Turn the flashlight off. Go to sleep." Obediently, Akira turned off his flashlight and put it on the bed stand.

The following night, his flashlight became a lighthouse, breaking the darkness. He quickly switched it off when he heard the door open. He knew it was his father; he could smell him in the dark and expected to hear "Akira!" Instead he felt a warm hand on his forehead and a pat on his shoulders, twice. Akira pretended to be asleep. Long after his father had quietly closed the bedroom door, Akira could still feel his father's warm hand. He was no longer afraid. The night no longer held mysteries.

That was 83 years ago.

Today he lay in bed with no shadows playing in the dark. There was no need for a flashlight. He had learned to bring those he loved close to him. He had sent a photo of himself wearing his biggest smile to his picture bride in Hiroshima, hoping it would bring her to him. It did. At times the light had dimmed as it would, but he had managed to keep it going. He knew the battery of his heart was growing weaker. Akira felt at peace now, listening to the hushed voices around him.

"I'm going to miss his smile," one of them said.

"Remember how we used to fight to sit on his lap? He would make us play Jan-ken-po to see who sat first."

"Yeah, you used to cheat." Laughter filled the room.

Akira withdrew his hand from the ones clasping his. The voices in the room stopped.

He reached out again. The voices resumed. He liked the sense of control it gave him. Akira knew he would soon be in the dark. For the moment, he thoroughly enjoyed being under the tent with his flashlight. ▩

Once There Was a Kapoho

Dear Frances,

From my experiences in archaeology, volcanic ash falls and lava flows are the paradoxical destroyers and preservers. Whatever has survived of your old home, including foundations, carbonized wood and any remnants of the items your family had to burn in the backyard, will still be preserved within the Earth, even after the pyramids are gone.

Charles Pellegrino

Dear Dr. Charlie,

You inspired me to return to Kapoho. I thought there was nothing there, but look at all the shock cocoons I found in my dig. I started at my grandmother's house and dug down to 1941. And I thought there was nothing there.

Frances

Fire goddess Pele was venturing out in a creep, like spilled molasses, toward the village of Kapoho, a small, quiet, peaceful plantation village, thirty miles east of Hilo.

A pungent, rotten-egg-like sulfur stench combined with the smell of burning wood floated over Kapoho on gray wisps of smoke, raining black ash over cars, over rooftops and on windows. The village, like dice in a gambler's hand, shook and rattled. The lava flow burned everything in its path, slowly and with excruciating efficiency—sugarcane, ʻōhiʻa and guava trees—feeding its red, hungry mouth as it crept toward Kapoho. My grandmother's house, a lone sentry a few miles from the village, stood next in line.

My grandmother—or Oba-ban, as I called her—stood on the porch of her house, which rose six concrete steps from the ground. She saw shapes like Rorschach inkblots in red, shooting up into the sky, more than ten miles away. She didn't see any reflected danger in other faces. Instead, she shouted to my uncle, "I can see the lava so clearly from here. *Tashika mon.*" She didn't know that what she was calling "spectacular" was going to cover her house in less than twelve hours.

This was not the first time that fire would destroy her possessions. The first conflagration was created by her own hands in 1941. She had darted around her house like a moth caught in the chimney of a kerosene lamp, hurriedly grabbing anything that looked Japanese: vases, scrolls, fans, rice bowls, kimono-clad dolls, canned Japanese pickles. She tossed them into a small bonfire in her backyard. What couldn't be burned she buried in a shallow grave.

"*Hayaku, hayaku,*" she muttered to herself. "Hurry, hurry." Her head kept turning toward the road, looking for MPs. Only yesterday, Mr. Miura, the Japanese-language teacher, had been taken away to an internment camp somewhere on the mainland. If she could only bury her face. She was safe for now; no one would accuse her of being disloyal. She turned toward the bonfire. Nothing could touch her now. She didn't know that a force stronger than MPs would destroy everything she owned in 14 years.

My brother Paul was the first in our family to respond. He knew exactly what to do. His teenage friends rushed over in a car and shouted at him, "Come on, let's go! Eruption! Eruption! It's near your grandmother's house!" Paul grabbed a few empty Coke bottles and jumped into the backseat of the car, and they sped away toward the flow.

Yes, toward the flow, because this was what we did. During past eruptions, we had taken our jackets and thermoses filled with hot coffee and tea and driven out to the rim of Halema'uma'u Crater with hundreds of others to watch Pele's fireworks shooting into the sky, higher than the Empire State Building. The deafening roar of the boiling lava had made conversation difficult, and the smell of sulfur had filled our nostrils. Why would this eruption be any different to Paul?

Paul and his friends ran right past my grandmother standing on the porch. At the flow site, they dipped long guava branches into the hot lava, quickly lifted them out and dropped the clumps of lava on the ground near their feet. The lava cooked quickly, showing patches of black on its surface.

They ignored the scorching 2000°F heat. "Quick! Press the bottle in! Quick! Press the bottle in!" someone yelled. They took their empty Coke bottles and pressed the bottoms of the bottles into the lava. After the lava cooled, they removed the bottles, which had left a round, shallow impression in the cooled rock.

"Wow, check these out. Perfect ashtrays!"

"Hey, let's go sell these to the tourists in Hilo. We can get rich."

"Yeah, we can call them Pele's ashtrays."

"Naah, we don't want to get bad luck. You know what they say: people all get sick or get into accidents when they take rocks and sand out of Hawai'i."

"But we're safe since we not taking them out. Let the tourist get bad luck."

The villagers, so used to earthquakes and eruptions, remained relatively calm. News of the flows was as erratic as Pele. She taunted them, sometimes moving toward the village, sometimes backing off and going another way.

"Naah, we're safe," some said. "The lava won't come to the village." But when news that my grandmother had been forced to abandon her porch and that her house was now under lava became certain, the National Guard trucks began to rumble into the village and evacuate people in earnest.

Villagers loaded their household belongings into trucks and any other available vehicles. Friends and relatives from other towns began to arrive. Bedding, clothes, photographs, family treasures; whatever their hands could grab was tossed into the backs of trucks and cars. A young girl near the gate to her house watched strange men heaving furniture into the backs of trucks. She began to cry and clutched her doll closer to her chest.

In the midst of this unplanned, instant evacuation, Pele still ruled. "Pele is good to us after all," a villager said. "She warned us with earthquakes before she sent the lava. Look at how much time she's giving us to evacuate. See, no one was killed or hurt by her eruption." No one dared to curse her out of sheer fear or belief.

Oba-ban, on the other hand, was not held in Pele's good graces, if the rumors that were spreading faster than the fingers of lava snaking their way over Kapoho had any inkling of truth to them.

Oba-ban ran a neat, clean house. Her Buddhist altar never lacked fresh flowers or burning incense. She wasn't the type of woman who wore an apron and baked cookies for me. An immigrant from Hiroshima, she had buried two husbands in Hawai'i long before I was born, and she'd been left to raise seven children. I eavesdropped once on my parents speculating that my grandmother could have escaped from a husband when she emigrated to Hawai'i. Whatever history she possessed, it remained sealed in the deep lines on her face. If she heard any of these stories surrounding her house and why it was destroyed, she added them to her silence. Life meant survival to her, and she was seldom seen sauntering; there was no time for gossip and rumors.

Oba-ban was a no-nonsense woman. She seldom showed affection. She once slapped her chopsticks on my knuckles during dinner and scolded in a tone that implied her disbelief that a granddaughter of hers could be so ill bred. "What is the meaning of this? Nicely brought up girls don't hold rice bowls with two fingers!"

She had caught me holding my rice bowl up to my face with my thumb and forefinger to get rice into my mouth, pushing the grains of rice with my chopsticks. I quickly held my rice bowl properly, using the palm and five fingers of my left hand. But more importantly than learning good manners, I had discovered a way to rile her. Occasionally, I purposely became that not-so-well-brought-up granddaughter by holding my rice bowl by the rim with my thumb and forefinger. It's not an easy task to eat rice out of a bowl held by two fingers; it can be as awkward as balancing on two homemade stilts. But it was worth her chopsticks.

The other slap from her chopsticks was directed to my natural-born instinct to be left-handed. "No nice family will accept you as a bride if you eat with your left hand. Nothing is more clumsy and graceless than a girl eating and writing with her left hand!" So I was forced to eat and write with my right hand and remained unmarried.

Oba-ban could be harsh, but when no one came to defend her on the day that Pele took her house, I felt that the people passing on these stories were not so kind. My mother had a simple explanation: Oba-ban must have refused fruit and water to the people who were telling these stories.

"Your grandma got bachi for making Pele mad," they told me.

"Yeah, I heard that Pele asked her for some of the fruit from her yard, and she refused to give her any. I heard that she didn't even give Pele a glass of water."

"No wonder her house was the first to go."

"Pele didn't give her time to save anything."

"I guess she didn't recognize that the old woman was Pele."

I grew up hearing about Pele taking the form of an old woman, walking around the Volcano and Puna areas with her white dog. "Be kind to old women," we were told. "They could be Pele." My grandmother evidently didn't believe this.

The spookiest Pele story was told by lone male drivers on the Volcano road late at night:

"I looked in my rearview mirror and saw a woman, young and beautiful, sitting in the backseat. She had long black hair and was dressed in red. I turned my head, wondering how she got in my car. But when I turned to look, there was no one there. I got chills and got out of there fast."

My family evacuated to my aunt's house in Mountain View. Other villagers were scattered to different parts of the Islands, staying with relatives and friends. The radio crackled with misinformation so often that the air became a fertile place for rumors.

"Did you hear? Someone saw Pele facing Pāhoa. I think Pāhoa is going to be next."

"Someone saw Pele walking toward Hilo."

"Maybe we should evacuate to Honolulu."

The rumors grew with the growing anxieties and fear. Even my grandmother's behavior became part of the history of Pele's anger.

I was away in college, buried under my studies to get pidgin out of my mouth on my way to becoming a famous writer. I had no way of learning firsthand what was happening to my family and friends in or out of Kapoho. That panic later turned into anger as I shot bombastic arrows into my speech class. Instead of giving my prepared speech that day, I tossed it aside and gave vent to some improvised rage.

"Kapoho, my hometown, is being destroyed by lava as I stand here. In the snack bar downstairs, in the media and in conversations among many of you who have taken helicopter rides to view the eruption, I hear you saying things like 'spectacular,' 'awesome' and even 'inspiring.' The camera lenses and the firsthand sightings from low-flying helicopter rides only show Pele's fire. That can be awesome. Spectacular, even, if Kapoho were just a piece of dirt, a nowhere place that nobody cares about. But Kapoho is where I grew up.

"My family has evacuated to my aunt's house. I was there last weekend when my father's name shrieked from the radio to identify the next house that was destroyed. My father's response made me feel afraid for him as I watched his disbelief. I was afraid that his mind could crack like the land beneath our house, cracked wide open by earthquakes.

"My father looked at us and said, 'That can't be me. That must be another Sadame Kakugawa.' It was spooky to hear him say that.

"My father is a simple plantation worker. He earns minimum wage to support our family of seven and send me to school. We depend on our thirteen acres of cane land to pay off our debts. Losing our home would just kill him.

"When my mother told him, 'It is your house. There is no other Sadame Kakugawa,' my father just sat there. I could see him looking for some way out. The hardest thing I had to watch that sad day was his resignation. He said, 'If Pele wants my house, she can have it.'

"And that's just one story, mine. There's a village full of stories like this, and the saddest part is that there isn't even a village anymore. You want spectacle? There's a spectacle for you."

I sat abruptly down. At least one person had heard me that day, because for the rest of the year, my lunches were paid for at the snack bar. All I knew about my benefactor was that he was a veteran.

We had known we were living on top of a live volcano. The steam rising from small fissures that were under our house would rot some of my father's fishnets.

"I think Pele lives under our house," my father would say. Scientifically, it was a canary.

Pele was warning us, but we never gave it a thought. We took it for granted; the dampness and the smell of rotten eggs were as normal and natural as the wrigglers or the tiny fragments of stones caught in the Bull Durham tobacco bags that hung around our tap to filter water from the wooden water tanks.

My father's relationship with Pele was personal. He often went fishing at night and returned in the early hours of the morning. When he returned within an hour, we knew there was a story that he would tell us later.

"I was about to throw my net when something told me to turn around. I saw this old woman with long white hair, standing behind me on the rocks. She had no feet. I knew it was Pele warning me that the waves were too rough and dangerous, so I picked up my net and said, 'Thank you, Pele' and came home."

My father was not the only family member who respected Pele.

When I taught in Michigan, I was invited to speak to various groups about life in Hawai'i. Once a student asked, "Do you believe in gods and goddesses in Hawai'i?"

For a split second, I wanted to say "No." Back then, people still believed that Hawaiians wore grass skirts and lived in huts. If I said "Yes," we'd look like uncivilized savages. If I said "No," I'd be standing in Oba-ban's shoes at the top of some porch. I finally said, "Yes, I believe in Pele, the goddess of fire who lives in our volcanoes." In their eyes, I set our civilization back a hundred years at least.

Eventually, my family rented a small house in a plantation village about eight miles away from Kapoho. We lived there for a year before we relocated to another site. The Territory of Hawai'i had opened "state land" in Pāhoa, seven miles away. There was a public auction.

My parents and former neighbors were determined to save their neighborhood. They selected adjoining lots. My mother started the bidding on a three-acre lot for the starting price, set at $300.

Some relative from Hilo entered the bidding with his own bid. The price continued to go up. Mr. Hara, a store proprietor, urged my mother to bid to the end. "Keep bidding. I'll loan you the money."

Other neighbors were also bid against by out-of-town investors. One neighbor stood up and said, in a voice shaking with rage, "Shame on you for bidding. This is for the evacuees who lost their houses and lots. What are you doing here, messing up our auction? Shame on you." The bidding war continued. Our property was bought for $3,000. The story of this auction was told and retold by my parents for years.

Pele left many mysteries in her path. She sometimes destroyed homes and left the outhouses standing. She destroyed one neighbor's house but spared the one next to it. The villagers had a simple explanation: Pele saved the homes of the good and destroyed the homes of the selfish and the bad. Of course, only the villagers with homes still standing would make such claims. Pele had flowed around a thin three-wire fence at the Kapoho lighthouse and left its beacon, which had been shining since World War II, untouched. Other places here and there were similarly and mysteriously unscathed.

My father needn't have doubted Pele's generosity after all. When we returned to Kapoho, the house was, as he'd insisted, still standing as well. They must have meant some other Kakugawa. The large crack that had appeared under our house had disappeared, and the house was tilted at a funny angle. I stood in the living room and felt off balance, like being on the *Titanic,* half sunken and ready to sink.

We couldn't live there anymore, of course. There was no Kapoho. My father had given two acres of his cane land to Pele.

A year after the eruption, the Red Cross lifted our house by parts from its foundation and moved it to its new home in Pāhoa. The day the house was moved, I took one last walk around the lot, looking at the "under house" where my father used to hang his nets. Off to the side was a perfect row of Pele's ash-trays. So Paul and his friends had spared the tourists from Pele's wrath.

Joe was left standing, too. Joe was the town's hoodlum, the bad guy who couldn't be trusted even in broad daylight. Joe was the defiant boy who had dropped out of school at 16, hung out at the pool hall and smoked cigarettes in front of the grocery store, eyeing the girls who had come to do their shopping. I'd had one encounter with Joe.

One afternoon, I was on the porch when he stopped his car, rolled down his window and asked, "Hey, what you reading?"

I showed him *Fahrenheit 451* and explained, "It's science fiction, about a place in the future where they ban and burn books."

He laughed, "Maybe I should move there."

"You might enjoy this book. I got it from the bookmobile."

Our visit was cut short by my father, who had returned from work. His face told Joe that his visit was over. To me, he said, "You shouldn't be seen in his company."

Joe doesn't know how he helped me get my first college A in English 100. After the evacuation, I wrote about him in an essay titled, "In the Base, There Is Good."

Joe was one of the last to leave Kapoho. He stayed behind to help families load their cars and trucks with their belongings. He and three other men lifted a car that was stalled in the roadway so that others could drive through. He lifted a little crying girl and handed her to her mother, giving the girl a reassuring smile. Unlike my grandmother's story, Joe's story returned us to the basic human values needed during times of physical destruction.

As if losing one's possessions hadn't been heartache enough, the fire insurance companies ignored the insurance claims sent in by their clients, who had expected to be covered.

"Your policy is for fire, but eruption is an act of God, so your policy doesn't apply here," the insurance companies argued. "It wasn't the fire, it was the lava, which is an act of God, that burned your house down." One house simply exploded into flames without being touched by lava. "You are not covered for acts of God."

Pele did for the people of Kapoho what politicians had been promising for years. One senator's promise had played like a broken record every election year.

"If elected," he had shouted, "I will pave the road to Kapoho, I will light all your homes with electricity and all water tanks will be gone. You will have flush toilets instead of outhouses!"

When the Red Cross moved our house by parts to Pāhoa, it was a time of disaster, and we accepted whatever awaited us as our "new" home. The original house had had a porch two steps off the ground. It had been the gathering place for neighborhood kids and adults. It was here that we sat and talked story until the sun went down. It was here that I wrote my poems, tried my first cigarette, puffing out smoke like Bette Davis, and devoured romantic novels. The porch was where we returned to, like homing pigeons, at the end of the day.

That porch was gone with the rest of Kapoho, but a new porch now rose nine steps from the ground, with a panoramic view of ʻōhiʻa trees and the rooftops of neighbors. A white railing wrapped its arms around the porch, and two tiny gates without latches opened inward, just like the old. And for the first time since its construction, our house was lighted by electricity. The outhouse and water tanks remained in Kapoho.

Kapoho had been a breeding ground for dreams for anyone whose world was seen through Sears catalogs and storybooks. To pass the time before my escape, I'd slid down her grassy hills on cardboard boxes, read romantic novels in her mango trees and walked barefooted in her cane fields to look for mountain apples. I'd swum and nearly drowned many times in Warm Springs, her natural freshwater pool, and fished for goldfish in Green Lake. I'd made pipes out of young guavas: dug out the pulp, filled them with dried leaves, stuck a reed through the guava and smoked like those Hollywood stars. I'd body-surfed in her turbulent waves at Pohoiki and written poems while watching waves burst into suds against the rocks. I'd invited myself into homes to talk story with adults to pass my long summer months.

As if possessing radar, I knew exactly when our neighbor Amy was cooking pig's feet or beef bone soup. I'd be right there in her kitchen, watching her cook while we talked story. She made the best soup and told the spookiest ghost stories, which made me afraid of the dark. My worm and snake phobias probably originated in her kitchen.

"Once upon a time," Amy would begin, "there was a very poor family. They had a blind daughter who wanted to eat spaghetti. But they were so poor that they couldn't afford such foods, since all they had to eat were fish from the ocean and vegetables from their garden. The little girl cried and cried, so one day, the mother dug in the garden and gathered a bowl of earthworms. She poured tomato sauce over them and fed the girl. The girl said it was the best spaghetti she had ever eaten."

Mrs. Nakamura was proprietor of the Nakamura store, made famous by *Life* and *Look* magazines during the eruption. Her kitchen was also on my route. Sometimes I'd help her behind the cash register. When her son was drafted, Mrs. Nakamura, with tears in her eyes, said, "I feel a strong gust of wind came and left." "I know," I said, even though I had no idea what she meant.

Long after the eruption, she said, "I thank Pele for forcing us to retire. If not for Pele, I would still be working at the store instead of being retired here at this beach house."

When I wanted a Pepsi, my friend Sammy's house was the place. I'd nod when Sammy's mother asked, "Do you want a Pepsi?" She would then pour warm Pepsi into a white porcelain coffee cup. Sammy's mother told some of the scariest Hawaiian ghost stories. In one, a hand flew through the window to choke her. In another, strange music was heard in the middle of the night. "Probably menehunes," she explained, "walking over old Hawaiian graves."

The saddest story came from the sister of a little boy:

"We went to the airport to see my brother. I would see him only once a year. He moved away when he was eight. My family and I saw the plane land and slowly turn right in front of us. I pressed my face against the window to check each window, one by one. I strained to see which window would have a face.

"Finally I saw his face. He wasn't waving back, so I knew he couldn't see us. The plane stopped. I waved, and the tears rolled down my face. He was looking at me. He had grown since I last saw him. I heard my mother say, 'I can't recognize him anymore.' My brother waved with one hand.

"After about ten minutes, the plane taxied down the runway and took off."

Her brother never returned home from Moloka'i. There was no cure for leprosy, and there was no treatment except isolation.

This was the Kapoho that now lies under tons of lava—the one that I had plotted my great escape from for many years. But as it turned out, Pele had her own plans.

Pele is still relentless and continues to remind us of her presence now and then with earthquakes and eruptions. Even the smallest earthquake causes a state of panic as I wait for the few seconds of uncontrollable shaking to stop. A few seconds feel like long minutes. I live with the memory of a fall from the second floor to the ground at Pāhoa High and Intermediate School during one major earthquake. My hands were torn from the railing, and down the stairs I went, one step at a time, on my buttocks. There was nothing I could do but give in to the quake.

To add to my trauma, I heard the principal shouting, "Hold on! Damn you! Hold on!"

The next day, the school secretary refused to let me see the principal after I explained why I wanted an appointment. "I want an apology from him for yelling and swearing at me yesterday."

The secretary shook her head at me and said, "He was afraid for your safety. That's why he yelled." I still panic at the slightest stir.

Our home was now seven miles away from Kapoho. Years after our relocation, a new series of earthquakes began to appear on the seismograph, centered in the area of Pāhoa.

"Pele was seen facing Pāhoa." This unnerved many former residents of Kapoho, who, now living in Pāhoa, wondered whether Pele was going to pay them a second visit. I was living at home then.

The tremors grew more constant. My Uncle Jun from Hilo appeared in our yard with his truck. He was the uncle who had evacuated us during an air raid after Pearl Harbor. We could always count on Uncle Jun to be there.

"The radio said there's going to be an eruption. You must evacuate," he called out.

"No, no," my parents said. "It won't come. Not a second time."

"Uncle Jun drove all the way from Hilo," I argued. "We should really go with him. Otherwise, he came for nothing." My parents stood firm and brushed aside my concern for Uncle Jun.

I got on his truck anyway. I was the only evacuee from Pāhoa that day. Riding through the village, I saw residents sitting on benches in front of stores, watching the traffic pass. Nobody seemed to be in a hurry or anything.

"Hideko, you're the smart one," my uncle said.

I spent the day at Uncle Jun's house. He drove me back to Pāhoa later that evening.

Kapoho's landscape is gone, but the heartbeat that was Kapoho still lives under the megatons of lava rocks and in my middle name, Hideko. In Kapoho, I was always "Hideko." My English name, Frances, was reserved for school and places outside of Kapoho.

Today, when I hear "Hideko," I know immediately that it's a voice from Kapoho. It feels as though a piece of lava crust has suddenly split open to reveal my village name inside.

I recently spoke to 800 students at Waiākea Elementary School in Hilo. One third grader mentioned my visit to her grandmother, Lehua. When I answered the phone that evening and heard, "Hideko?", I was back in Kapoho again. Lehua, her brother Sammy, and their family and ours had spent most of our summers and holidays together.

"Hideko" still appears at many of my book signings and lectures. When I hear "Hideko, remember me?", I look for a Kapoho face. At funeral services for someone from Kapoho, past residents will attend merely because "It's a Kapoho funeral." Stronger than any Kīlauea magma is this humanity of ours, holding on to a place that no longer exists except in her people.

Dear Frances,

It's always interesting to think about how many layers of our civilization are buried under lava and ash. It's one of the things they keep missing on the History Channel's "Life After People." One-third of Pompeii is still under the ash, and two-thirds of its infinitely better preserved sister city of Herculaneum. The buried city of Thera (under the volcanic Isle of Santorini) is mostly hidden under the rock and ash after 3,600 years, and if humanity were to disappear utterly, these homes and streets would still be sleeping within the Earth long after the pyramids and our tallest skyscrapers are eroded away without trace.

Charles P

Dear Dr. Charlie,

The last generation of children born in Kapoho are now in their 70s and 80s. Soon no one will be calling me Hideko, but as you have kept humanity alive under Pompeii, the Titanic, Hiroshima, Nagasaki and the Twin Towers, waiting under Kapoho may be stories for future excavators. This gives me hope for the future. The future may mean tourist hotels and shops and even a quaint little shop over my grandmother's old house. It doesn't matter, Kapoho will always be there, and I'll be digging for new treasures and new shock cocoons. Maybe I'll even hear someone calling my name, Hideko. You told me once that you were going to turn me into a literary archaeologist. I think you just did, for a few layers anyway. ▣

Hideko

A Postscript

On the U.S. Geodetic Survey's Hawaiian Volcano Observatory Web site, "The 1960 Kapoho Eruption of Kilauea Volcano, Hawai'i" covers the Kapoho eruption with photos and facts. My poem "Once There Was a Kapoho," written for the first reunion of Kapoho residents, appears on the site at http://hvo.wr.usgs.gov/kilauea/history/1960Jan13/kakugawa.html and is reproduced here.

Once there was a Kapoho
Where children played barefooted
Until the evening sun disappeared
And kerosene lamps and gas lamps
Beckoned each child home.

Once there was a Kapoho
Where outhouses and water tanks
Prominently stood as sentry guards
And 'ohi'a firewood sent signals above rooftops,
Announcing a hot furo for the tired and the toiled.

Once there was a Kapoho
Where mothers pumping sewing machines
Marked the end of summer;
Homemade clothes and one-strapped schoolbags
For the first of September.

Once there was a Kapoho
Without television but battery-run radios
For "The Romance of Helen Trent,"
Dr. Malone and Arthur Godfrey.

Once there was a Kapoho
Without washing machines
But wooden washboards against concrete tubs
And slippery, muddy denims
Boiled in Saloon Pilot cans.

Once there was a place
Without shopping malls and Liberty House
But catalogs from Sears and Montgomery Ward,
Dream-makers, before turning into a Charmin or MD.
Once there was Christmas without lights.

Yes, once there was a place
So simple and free
Where children swam in Warm Springs
And fished in Green Lake,
Played marbles and Ojame
And Steal Steal Stone.

Once there was a place
Where life went on without questions.
Sons went off to war,
Teachers taught the 3 Rs,
Parents were the PTA
And children pledged allegiance.

Yes, once there was such a place
Until Madame Pele said, "No more!"
And scattered all the children
Like stars in the universe,
Echoing Thomas Wolfe,
"You can't go home again."

Glossary

Bachi divine retribution
Bakatare stupid
Daikon white Japanese radish
Furo bath
Futon Japanese cotton-filled quilt
Haole Caucasian
Hapa-haole half Caucasian
Hayaku hurry
Issei first generation Japanese
Jan-ken-po paper, stone, scissors game
Juzu Buddhist prayer beads
Kalbi Korean barbecue
Mauka toward the mountains
Mochi rice cake
Moxa mugwort herb
Nisei second generation Japanese American born of issei parents
Nishime Japanese dish prepared with chicken and special vegetables
Oba-ban grandmother
Obon Buddhist dance festival honoring the dead
Ōhi'a native Hawaiian tree (metrosideros polymorpha) producing lehua blossoms
Ojame game played with beanbags
Pansit Filipino noodle dish
Sansei third generation Japanese American born of nisei parents
Sashimi raw fish
Shikata ganai It can't be helped.
Shoyu soy sauce
Steal Steal Stone in Kapoho, a children's game of tag using a rock
Sushi Japanese rice rolls
Tashika mon spectacular
Tennou-heika-sama The Very Honorable Emperor
Ume pickled plum
Yaito burning moxa on specific places on the body as a cure for certain illnesses
Yokatta It was good.
Zori rubber slippers

About the Author

Born and raised in the village of Kapoho on the Big Island of Hawai'i, Frances H. Kakugawa is an author of ten books who has received numerous awards from literary and family caregiving organizations—among them, the Hawai'i Book Publishers Association, Northern California Publishers & Authors, Mom's Choice Awards, California Writers Club and Hawai'i Pacific Gerontological Society. She has also been recognized by the Hawai'i Japanese Women's Society Foundation as one of the Outstanding Women of the 20th Century in Hawai'i. Frances has taught at schools in Michigan, Micronesia and Hawai'i, where she was a curriculum writer, teacher trainer and lecturer in the College of Education at the University of Hawai'i at Mānoa. She currently gives lectures, workshops and readings to schools and community groups nationwide on the subjects of caregiving, teaching, writing and poetry, and she also facilitates a writing support group for caregivers in Sacramento, California, where she lives.